Love & Loss shows

Set free the Voice o...
Uncover your life-force energy
Use your imagination

In *Love & Loss* the reader is confronted with a raw, honest account of the author's own lived experience of love and loss and her attempts to make sense of the experience through the act of 'creative therapeutic writing'. This is a brave, highly personal testimony, but it will be a rare reader who does not encounter here a reflection of some dimensions of their own experience and – critically – a toolkit that might just unlock a deeper understanding of what makes us who we are.

Jeremy Page, editor: *The Frogmore Papers*

What is immediately apparent in reading this book is the accessible and honest telling. The invitation for the reader is to write and cultivate personal wisdom. Writing is not just seen as an activity, but as an archetypal character – a cartographer who allows us to learn and draw our own map for good living. 'Why should I invade my own privacy?' Monica Suswin asks in a humorous way. And the response is clear: our own vulnerability, written down, but then also edited with care becomes a gift for others who all share the human experience of love, loss, and the precious insights that articulating lived experience brings.

Dr Reinekke Lengelle, visiting professor:
Universities of Alberta, Athabasca, The Hague

Direct, honest and emotionally sensitive *Love & Loss* is a candid exploration. Monica Suswin finds an intimate voice for the therapeutic exploration of her experience and engagement with writing. *Love & Loss* is also alive with creative ideas for writers and workshop leaders of all kinds.

Dr Lisa Dart, writer

Love & Loss

creative therapeutic writing
on
relationships.

MONICA SUSWIN

CABIN PRESS

This book is dedicated to
Dr Ian Marshall

1931–2011

Once Zhuangzi dreamt he was a butterfly, a butterfly flitting and fluttering around, happy with himself and doing as he pleased. He didn't know he was Zhuangzi. Suddenly he woke up and there he was, solid and unmistakable Zhuangzi. But he didn't know if he was Zhuangzi who had dreamt he was a butterfly, or a butterfly dreaming he was Zhuangzi. Between Zhuangzi and a butterfly there must be some distinction! This is called the Transformation of Things.

attributed to Zhuangzi (Chuang Tzu) Chinese philosopher,
fourth century BC from *The Complete Works of Chuang Tzu*
by Burton Watson (translator) © 1968: p. 49, Columbia University Press
Reprinted with permission of the publisher

Love is all you need
The Beatles, 1967

Contents

Acknowledgements

I am grateful to those I have loved and still love, and those who have loved me and still love me. I am blessed to have the particular loves in my life which have given rise to the writing in this book.

As always I am indebted to my friends: Liz Bahs, Alison Bell, Jill Hall who have read and responded to early drafts of my writing. Paul Luffman at Short Run Press has been wonderfully patient as I have learnt the intricacies of, and liaising about, typesetting. A big thank you to Tash Wales of CRTC Studios for photoshopping the colourful butterfly on the cover. I would like to thank Helen Stapleton for reasons she will understand. I am particularly grateful to Sarah Davies and my 'wave of energy' dancing partners who have given me the freedom to find and express my inner younger and playful self which complements my writing.

I want to record my gratitude to the late Ian Marshall who I met in my twenties; he was the first map-maker of my adult life, teaching me how to think and what it meant to take responsibility for myself: an important strategy underpinning creative and therapeutic writing. I also owe my understanding of psychotherapeutic principles and Jungian concepts to him. We were friends to the end of his life.

I am as always grateful to Mark Haughton who is a great supporter of my writing holding a compass wherever true north points and south, east and west as the needle swings. My greatest thanks go to my daughter and son-in-law who have produced a grandson, a creative project of truly lasting love.

My heartfelt thanks to Dr Gillie Bolton who has been a brilliant editor continuing her map reading of my endless drafts and always giving me new directions to follow. Sometimes neither of us knew where the writing was going but it certainly was going somewhere. She led and I have followed. I have led and she has followed. Both leading and following. Our joint work has arrived at its destination: this second mini-book.

Introduction

Ever since I was a teenager, I have one way or another been in the grip of Love. Love with a capital L. This book is about the versatility of creative therapeutic writing about both Love and Loss. Loss also with a capital L. Only with the hindsight of coming towards the other end of a long life am I able to write something which points to its mysteries and unfolding.

There is no mystery, however, to the loss of love. That hurts. Experiential writing has helped me deal with and express painful partings, and adjust to the Loss of Love and the ending of relationships. Writing has helped me separate out from strong feelings, yet still stay in touch with a loving self. Writing has proved to me that my heart is resilient and optimistic, and has shown me that Love is enduring beyond all other feelings. This book explores some of the ways writing has led me to that conclusion.

Sometimes I think of Writing (at times also with a capital W, as if a proper name) as a character in itself: a medium apart from myself which receives my inner feelings, absorbs and transforms them and leaves me refreshed and renewed. And then lands me somewhere else. This means I own myself in a different way, but still feel very much myself. Perhaps more so.

With so much writing, both creatively and therapeutically, I have experienced the unfolding of a more complex inner life. Even the final processes of bringing this writing to publication adds to a fuller and more rounded sense of myself. Allows me to accept and acknowledge how Love has shaped my life through writing poems, lyrical prose, ordinary prose, dialogues and unsent letters.

With reflection it looks as if I have at times wandered off piste with my theme. Yet this is the joy of the unknown adventure, going with an unerring trust of how Writing unfolds and reveals itself. If Writing were a character, I would think of a cartographer: one that has taken charge of their own life in this book. I feel I have been on a meander around a map of his or her own making.

Recently gender issues and gender identity have exploded into public awareness. But I am interested, however, in thinking about how my inner masculine self has become integrated with my female self. This concept stems from Jungian thinking about androgyny: the integration of male and female qualities in one individual. Jung was writing in another age when gender definitions were clearly identified in a way we no longer recognize. You will find notes in the appendix to deal with these kind of anomalies when they are not addressed within the chapters.

Love and the arousal of sexuality was the theme I thought I was writing about when setting out on this book. But very soon my writing led me to metaphors and ancient archetypes (another Jungian term). No map. No known destination. Yet the Writing found its own paths, and proved to be a great teacher about Love without trying to own or control it. Love, I have learnt, exists in its own right as an energy force ebbing and flowing through me, and flowing between me and others.

Writing has helped me towards a wisdom late in life, enabling me to grasp a cautious following of Love and a respect for its fluctuations. I let go when it is no longer there and hold on when it is real.

Many literary styles come into this kind of writing. And all sorts of ways of explaining: *creative and therapeutic, exploratory and experiential* are some of the words to describe this genre. Another phrase is *Writing for Wellbeing*. (Creative non-fiction and autoethnographic writing are also recognized terms in academic circles.) I may use different phrases throughout this book. They all point in one direction: writing which helps us live our lives more fully and creatively. Certainly the writing of this book has done just that for me and has helped me come to terms with the quality of relationships in my life.

Writing helps resolve tricky areas in life. And sometimes Love is tricky indeed. This book is about my personal writing: writing which probed my inner self. Why on earth would I share this and invade my own privacy? There are several answers and explanations. I make a distinction between being the writer who pours everything onto the page, and evolving into an author who wants to publish. Much of my personal writing has been pared down to its essence, redrafted and edited so that it is suitable to be read by others. I hope what has been helpful for me may also be helpful for you the reader.

Exploratory and experiential writing feels like my natural home. The approach I take to creative writing with a therapeutic angle reflects my practical training in humanistic psychotherapy in the seventies. At that time it was normal for practice to be far more grounded in personal experience than an academic or theoretical framework. I like experimenting with writing and that is what I do: I will take you through the steps of my own writing processes which have allowed me to positively transform how I think and feel.

Much of this writing was done so long ago that its original emotional impact is no longer inside me. The circumstances and feelings are in the words on the page.

The paradigm that underpins this book may not be apparent, but is loosely based on what has become known as the Hegelian* principle of thesis, antithesis and synthesis (although this was not the terminology the German philosopher Hegel used himself). I find this helpful in looking at how we relate to others: how identification with a significant other may initially involve a kind of merging, then a separating out as the differences between two people become apparent. Finally, if a relationship develops sufficiently, the third stage of relating, based on respect for individual separateness of selves, meet in true connection.

In *The Quantum Self* Danah Zohar, (co-authored with her husband Dr Ian Marshall), explained how relationships develop in the beginning between mother and baby (fuse), then in adulthood how patterns may mirror this early learning and go through the stages of fuse-split-connect (1990: pp. 118-9).

Writing also perhaps goes through the Hegelian three stages. In the early stages of writing I am fused with my material. During redrafting I separate out from the original material and content. After those two stages are completed, I put on my editorial hat for the final draft and start to relate to my writing as if a reader. (My real-life editor steps in during the last two stages with a fresh pair of eyes and her own mindset and skills.) These vital stages of writing prepare the material for publication, not necessarily in neat progression as the last two stages go back and forth a bit with much redrafting. In relationships we also move in and out of phases: yet it is a helpful paradigm.

Finally I connect with my writing through the completion of these three stages. In this particular book, I feel I may connect with you as my reader though a diverse and diffused sense of loving for humankind as a whole. We are driven by our life forces beyond sexuality itself and this can be expressed through a passion for all manner of things. Mine happens to be writing.

THE SERIES

This book: *Love & Loss: creative therapeutic writing on relationships* is the second of a series. Each of the four books stands alone on a different theme, and includes:

  * Writing from a dream image extended creatively and therapeutically.

* Writing which has been invaluable for a range of life issues through my own lived experiences.

The dream in Chapter 1 gave rise to the phrase and title of Chapter 2: *Erotic Alert*. The exploratory writing here hints at the potential elements of the romantic phase of relationship. The example is speculative, imaginative and improbable, but often in early romantic attraction psychological fusion with another is experienced. The fusion, however, turned out to be within myself which I explored with writing about androgyny. Chapter 3: *Raw Heart* shows how poems and narrative prose unravelled the letting go of one relationship, and separating out in my marriage. Chapter 4: *Butterfly* charts my own connections in a loving relationship with my daughter and a significant other through journal extracts and lyrical writing.

Love & Loss is for anyone who thinks exploring the huge subject of Love and relationships through writing will be helpful.

This book will be useful for practitioners in the helping professions by illuminating how *Writing for Wellbeing* may be a resource for those they seek to help.

If you are having issues with a relationship, or helping someone with a relationship problem, then the different ways of writing shown in this book might be good to try. Write within your own limits of comfort; crying can be a release and often accompanies emotional writing. Take responsibility for yourself and your needs. Seeking out the support of a practitioner in the healing arts or a trusted other can be beneficial at certain times to share issues, accompany you with whatever you are experiencing.

Each chapter ends with writing exercises based on my different styles and approaches to *creative and therapeutic writing*.

* Blogs can be read at: www.monicasuswin.wordpress.com

* An asterix in the text indicates more information in the Notes

CHAPTER 1

Dream Snatcher

THE ROYAL ROAD OF WRITING

In my diary which I write every morning, interspersed with rapid gulps of hot tea, I record my dreams if they strike me as more than a jumble of images. Sometimes I just write them up and leave it at that. Other times I may pursue a thread (snatch) of the dream, and then augment it with exploratory writing. There are times when my dreams feel just as vivid as daytime events, and just as real. I regard them as a rich part of my inner life: <u>the theatre of my mind</u>. ⭐

When I write from my own dreams, I use a range of creative therapeutic writing strategies. These help me to pay proper attention to the meanings I discover as they unfold from the writing. Scribbling quickly, to remember as much as possible, is usually how I record my dreams and often in the past tense. I choose the 'snatch', then rewrite in the present tense to bring the scene to life.

Sigmund Freud famously worked with his patients and his own dreams, calling the unconscious associations that arose in psychoanalysis as *the royal road to the unconscious*.* Carl Jung came to the conclusion that Freud led his patients away from their dreams into their neurosis and too specifically into sexual interpretations.* Jung wanted to make sense of the dream itself as a form, had a far broader canvas and disagreed with Freud's approach. By contrast, he believed a dream could be *a specific* *expression of the unconscious* and repeatedly said to his patients: *Let's get back to your dream. What does the dream say?* (Jung 1964, pp. 20-38).

By the late twentieth century, the understanding of dreams belonged far more to the dream-owner than to the expertise of a psychotherapist. The interpretation of dreams which gives rise to insights that *remain purely intellectual* may miss the experience of understanding with *lasting benefit for the dreamer because the feelings may have been bypassed* (Shohet 1985, pp. 30-31).* I learnt to explore my dreams in that felt experiential way through my training in humanistic psychotherapy* and specifically through a Gestalt approach.*

Although the dream which kick-started the *royal road of writing* in this book led to insights and some knotty layers of emotions, I also followed creative directions and diverse digressions to be found in later chapters.

Here is my original dream snatch:

IT ALL STARTS WITH A CUP OF COFFEE

A young man tells me the coffee from the percolator is finished. *Will I accept instant coffee?* I hardly ever drink instant coffee but I want my morning coffee so I agree and drink it quickly. By this time he tells me the real coffee is ready. He gives me a cup of coffee mounded with white froth. It looks divine. It tastes fantastic. It is the best cup of coffee I have ever seen or drunk.

A vivid dream scene had unrolled in my mind's eye as I wrote up this snatch the morning after a long rambling dream. I chose this one scene to explore further. The dream itself had started like this:

I was at a large family gathering in an Olympic size stadium. Then I was crossing a muddy garden to a big grand house. Everyone was sitting around tables in the garden polishing off a fry up. Morning buns and coffee were being served from a stall under an awning. I joined the queue.

This second piece is in the past tense because it had all happened during the previous busy night. The dream provided many images but I chose the snatch about the young man to work with. My first description about the cup of coffee at the stall was rewritten in the present tense; that gave the exchange immediacy. Every time I reread that scene, I find it comes alive and leaps into my mind.

I was intrigued this was the best cup of coffee I had ever been given so I continued to explore the significance of the young man giving me that dream cup of coffee. The thought of coffee, however, made me go and make myself a real cafetière of coffee to give myself authenticity. I drink coffee once a day mid-morning, and all else going on around me loses any significance at all when I am ready for that coffee. I got myself into my writing by starting with the here and now:

It is actually a very good cup of coffee. A real cup of coffee. The warmth spreads through my mouth, the taste is velvety smooth on my tongue, my stomach is satisfied and my taste buds are anticipating a Sunday morning brunch. Outside the sun has come out with autumnal light and my writing is coming on a treat. Bliss.

THE EXPLORATORY WRITE UP

Whilst enjoying my coffee and keeping in the present tense, I continued with my imaginative description, introducing some speech and interior monologue. I spoke the words silently in my head and then tried them out loud for effect:

> This is the best cup of coffee I have ever been given. *Thank you.* You are an attractive man. About thirty-something. Dark hair, several day's stubble growth.

That was pretty short though, so I went over the scene again with my eyes closed to visualize the young man more clearly and gave him space to speak back to me. Then some more description, not minding if I repeated myself. Repetition at this stage of exploration really helped me get into the flow of words. Here is what came:

> A young man gives me the best cup of coffee I have ever been given. *Thank you*, I say. And he replies: *a pleasure* and smiles at me. He smiles at me. What a nice young man. What a pity I am not thirty something and he could make himself a cup of coffee and we could find a table somewhere and have a quiet talk. And then go off for a walk into the countryside. I can see a path leading away from this crowded celebratory gathering. We could walk down this path. Talk. And be silent. And sit somewhere in a glade. And then I might stare into his eyes. And he might stare into mine.

This was a surprise write, rather soppy for my age. In my mind I may still feel in my thirties but in real life, at sixty-something, a young man was not going to walk down a green glade with me hand in hand. From best cup of coffee to taking thirty years off my age and having a romantic rendezvous. A pleasant few minutes writing. Was that rubbish? Was it meaningful? Certainly it was fantasy. A waking fantasy. Second best to a dream.

When my imagination freewheels and allows the drama to go on inside my head, I go into a sort of hypnagogic state like the liminal stage before or after sleep. Preparing myself to write, I quieten down, become aware of my breath, allow it to deepen, give myself over to slowness. Then I enter an imaginative space where I can relax into writing.

TAKING ON THE MASCULINE IDENTITY OF THE YOUNG MAN

Who was this young man? In a psychotherapeutic framework, certainly from a gestalt perspective, I needed to complete this exploration by taking on the voice of the young man and understand what he represented.

When I write in the first person pronoun, I create a far stronger relationship with my writing, I own my own words and identify with this 'I' Voice, even when it is from my imagination and given to a dream person. First of all I made an extremely simple self-explanatory statement as if from the young man, remembering to keep in the present tense:

I am thirty-two years old and a man. An older woman comes and asks me for a cup of coffee but I can only give her an instant quickly. A quick one. Is that what she wants?

I will magic up the most spectacular cup of coffee she has ever had. That will please her. I would like to please her. She smiles nicely. I wonder what she is thinking when she smiles at me. Maybe she likes me. I certainly like her. *Here is a better cup of coffee,* I say as I hand it to her. *Thank you,* she says. *A pleasure,* I say.

Light-hearted. Fun writing. It brought a smile to my lips.

Not long after this dream, I was in Morocco staying far in the south of the country. My camel guide was a real young man; he led me on a trip into the yellow sands of the desert.

Safe in the Sand Dunes

The March weather here is warm. I write this sitting on a wooden stool with a roughly woven seat, waiting for the kettle to boil. I am surrounded by a mud and straw brick wall built in the typical Moroccan pattern with squares and triangles and little turrets on the top. It must be about seven foot high. A black hen struts into my courtyard and then out again.

Karsch my Berber guide, a young man of twenty-five, led me on a camel called Abu deep into the desert to the sand dunes. I remembered the young man in my cup of coffee dream. As I ambled along sitting on the piled up rugs instead of a saddle, which was really comfortable, I reflected about young men in my life. I was quite alone with Karsch in the middle of the desert. A proper journey far from home and I was not a bit afraid. He talked to me about the young woman he loved. I felt perfectly safe with him. A young man as guide and protector.

My writing stemmed from that one tiny scene in the dream of waiting in the queue for a cup of coffee and ended with the realization that I often rely on the physical strength, and know-how or skills, of young men like Karsch who appear in my life.

Real young men, inner young men. What purpose might they have in my own life? For men the anima represents their inner female self. I find out more about my own animus (my inner male self)* in the next chapter which draws on Jungian concepts, now a hundred years old and attempt an answer to this question: *how can they still be relevant in the twenty-first century?*

Writing To Do

Dream Snatch

- Choose just one image or a vivid sequence
- Re-write in the present tense to bring the scene to life
- Allow your feelings to surface and include in your writing
- Allow the writing itself to become an experiential process

Dream Person

- Describe his or her physical appearance
- Pause and allow your breath to deepen
- Go with any changes of details that occur as you write
- Hold a conversation with the dream person
- Go over the dialogue and see if you can flesh it out

Writing To Do

Have Fun with Writing

Descriptions of everyday objects or activities, as if to a being from outer space, can produce irony. Here's an example:

The book is constructed of sequentially numbered sheets of paper, each sheet is scanned optically, registering information directly into your brain. A flick of the finger takes you to the next sheet. An optional bookmark accessory allows you to open the book to the exact place you left it in a previous session – even if the book has been closed.

adapted from *Built-in Orderly Organized Knowledge Device**
Marielle Cartier (1997)

- ♦ Describe going to bed and sleeping to someone who never sleeps
- ♦ Describe a dream to someone who never dreams
- ♦ Rewrite and exaggerate your description
- ♦ Pay attention to obvious details
- ♦ Relax into the flow of your writing
- ♦ Give yourself time-limits eg: 10 or 20 minutes
- ♦ Visit again another time and redraft

I always find if I allow some time to pass before rereading and rewriting, then images and phrases settle in my mind. Often when I wake in the morning, the imaginative and absurd come into my mind. Then I write more creatively.

Sleep can be a marvellous intervention. It sometimes sorts out my writing troubles, as well as waking me up with ideas. Often at four in the morning. I always have paper and pencil within easy reach.

(see: p. 33 about the flow of writing and freewriting)

Using the Five Senses

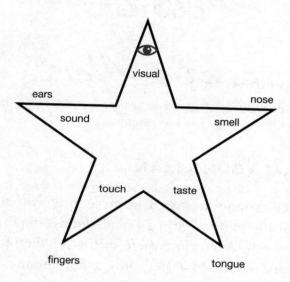

Some of the phrases I used in my dream snatch to bring it to life

A cup of coffee mounded with white froth
visual with implied taste and smell

the taste is velvety smooth
taste becomes tactile

several day's stubble growth
visual and feely words

A muddy garden to a big grand house
visual with contrasting images
visceral adjective for the garden

Thank you, she says. A pleasure, I say.
dialogue I can hear in my head

CHAPTER 2

Erotic Alert

MY DREAM YOUNG MAN

When the young man appeared in my cup of coffee dream and then romantically in my writing, I made an assumption about my younger inner self. Age: somewhere in the middle of my thirties. This suspension of reality lasted only a few minutes, but that is how the title of this chapter came about through my scribblings.

Eroticism is what I anticipated this chapter would be about. And I worried how I would write about sexuality in the context of my dream. How could I ignore what had been thrown up from my unconscious thoughts when writing about my lived life? I need not have been anxious. Although I took the risk of some explicit sexual writing, my writing soon led me off at various tangents into metaphor, symbols and archetypes. I grappled with out-of-date Jungian concepts of androgyny; I tackled Inner Voices and unravelled my responses to a D.H. Lawrence poem: *Snake*. And included my own poems about snakes, and one I had written in my thirties before I knew anything about writing poems.

My writing meandered around until I found what really lay at the foundation of *erotic alert*: the energy for life itself. I homed in on duality as the underlying theme throughout this chapter and made sense out of what had felt like a random exploration. This is a chapter where writing led and writing had its own wisdom to impart.

INNER YOUNG MAN

Starting then, naturally enough, with my own inner young man, I asked myself: *what were the qualities of young men I really wanted and could not have?*

I am the young man within Monica. In fact I am part of her. I inhabit her not through sex but by being inside her very being, inside her skin. I am the inner young man: the one to protect her; the one to be practical and the one to be strong.

A practical and strong inner young man. Immediately I thought about the concept of androgyny as found in Dr Carl Jung's theory of *anima* and *animus*. These were words he invented to describe the qualities of the opposite gender in a psychological sense for the biologically visible one. The original Jungian ideas about what belonged to the masculine and what belonged to the feminine are clearly outdated for our age.* Our thinking has turned towards a different approach to gender roles as we live them today.

My own approach then was not to look at the everyday particularity of social behaviour, but to focus on what masculinity might mean to me. To reflect on essence, not with the detail of roles within contemporary society. And so I made the terms of masculine and feminine relevant and fit for the purpose of my own writing in an archetypal sense.*

In that piece I saw the young man as protector: opposites balanced by age and gender. This fitted in with how Dr June Singer (1920–2004), an American Jungian analyst, wrote about awakening to the harmony of opposites (1989, p. 17).

The Masculine Principle and the Feminine Principle are both essential elements of everyone's psyche. They symbolize the opposites, like light and dark, soft and hard, yin and yang, work and rest, night and day. One cannot exist without the other, each gives the other meaning. If there were no night there could be no day.

Dr June Singer (1998)*

The role that dream young man played in my imaginative writing felt like a good interpretation and awareness of my androgynous self.* I am able to look after myself, but I have limitations I have to recognize. It reminds me of an instance when I was with a group of all ages at a bonfire night, a crowd of thousands moving up and down the streets. It seemed like everyone was towering above me as we made our way through the throngs with fire-crackers going off at our feet. One of the young men asked if I would like to take his hand and I took it gladly. And felt safer. Here the writing gave me an awareness that my own inner young man might give me more strength when I needed it. I often imagine him helping as I lug the supermarket bags out of the car up the grass bank to my front door.

Occasionally I strike lucky and the young boy who lives next door may be playing cricket or football with his friends on the wide grass verge in our road and he will come over and help me. It gives me great pleasure watching him grow up, getting taller with stylish haircuts as he becomes a teenager.

I make no bones about gaining much pleasure merely from looking at the beauty of young boys and men, as well as girls and women. I get a similar glow of pleasure when I look at the delicate petals of flowers, the sun glinting off an azure blue sea or the stars in the sky above the desert.

In Germaine Greer's book: *The Boy,* which has examples from art and sculpture, she wrote: 'Part of the purpose of this book is to advance women's reclamation of their capacity for and right to visual pleasure' (Greer 2003, p. 11). This all feels a million miles away from *erotic alert*; it is as much to do with the appreciation of my own delight for life with most of my life behind me now that

I am a grandmother, and observing the life-force of young people with the rest of their lives stretching ahead of them.

VOICES: GROWN UP & NAÏVE

Nevertheless I will address sexuality. For writing about a lived life, it really cannot be avoided. I do so with a fun piece and the feeling of being rather daring.

As I woke up one bright mid-winter morning pondering on the emotional and psychological integration of male and female consciousness, I wondered what sort of actual image this might conjure up. It is physiologically impossible to have two sets of complete and functioning reproductive organs nevertheless my imagination obliged with what is not possible in real life. Once this idea came into my head, an image presented itself immediately and I dared myself to write it. This scene unfolded in my mind with cinematic clarity:

And out of her sex the long perfect slender penis unfurls, tumescent and the inner and outer labia arrange themselves around the base like petals releasing the stamen. The inner opening remains just behind ready for gentle fingers and the penis.

Onto cushions one leans over, the palms spread flat; buttocks bared. The other comes close, smoothes the flesh with fingers tight as a fine comb teasing flesh until it trembles, s/he handles the slender penis and goes in; the first stands up, turns around. They hold onto each other like two halves of a fluted Grecian column until the second is also entered.

(2007)

Certainly I was taken aback for a minute or two when I realized the kind of image which came into my mind. Then more astonishment as the scene revealed itself to my inner eye. Then a permission to write it down. And ten years later in 2017, I am not shocked at all. My writing self had experienced a freeing up.

That I reflected was grown-up imaginative writing. In writing about the lived life rather than fiction, then sex is a subject best tackled privately. It is incredibly difficult to write about, but one I did not want to ignore. The next example took up the challenge I set myself. My solution was in using language at its simplest:

> That was a very nice day when they were both happy with each other; the day was hot and the man and the woman were sitting by the side of the lake. They were sitting at the eastern end, the mountain-side nearby, low bushes on the banks. No-one was around. The man got his own snake-thing out from the place where it was curled up. It is a good fit, she thought. It made her very pleased. Afterwards the man put it away and hid it.

Referring to the man and the woman helped me write about what I certainly did not want to have written with my 'I' Voice. It became a light-hearted piece, pretending for a kind of anonymity and innocence; also creating the similar distancing effect that the third person pronoun achieves. Because the writing allows for simple expressions alongside the implicit adult knowledge of sensuality, I call this my *naïve voice* (see: exercise box for more p. 74).

It is a good memory in writing. Not to be captured in a holiday camera shot. Better in some ways as it also brings back the feeling of the sun's heat on our skin.

THE SNAKE: METAPHOR AND SYMBOL

And I wished he would come back, my snake.
For he seemed to me again like a king,
Like a king in exile, uncrowned in the underworld,
Now due to be crowned again.

Snake by D.H. Lawrence
Taormina, 1923 *Stories, Essays and Poems* pp. 333-336

In the early twentieth century, activities behind closed bedroom doors were not mentioned in polite society. And when Lawrence's work was published with explicit writing about sex and sensuality, he was received with shock and condemnation.*

The poem: *Snake*, however, is a long narrative poem about a real snake Lawrence disturbed whilst living in the Italian countryside. A snake had come 'like a guest in quiet, to drink' at his water trough and 'flickered his two-forked tongue' as Lawrence waited, looked and thought.

This poem shows me so many aspects of writing: beautiful descriptive lines; visual evocative scenes, and how Lawrence placed his own complex self within this scene as observer and participant. All the way through Lawrence traces the conflict he experienced; both sides of an ambivalence about the snake's presence. He wavers between empathetic and instinctual feelings of admiration and 'the voices of my accursed human education' which tell him the snake 'must be killed'. That learnt voice half-heartedly won as he feebly threw a log at the snake as it disappeared down a hole, 'the earth-lipped fissure in the wall'.

Immediately this 'mean act' flipped him into regret – and at the same moment he saw the snake as 'one of the lords of life' making himself aware of his own 'pettiness'. In the penultimate stanza,

Lawrence elevated the snake to a state of majesty: 'uncrowned in the underworld'.

In its own body the snake carries a duality with its poisonous fanged tongue but its venom has enzymes which can heal. In Lawrence's poem there is a different two-edged symbolic meaning; one held in the ambivalence and conflict he experienced. The real fear came from the power of his educated mind, whilst his instinctual feelings veered towards admiration and appreciation for the snake.

One step into a further interpretation I make is the more abstract metaphorical meaning that the snake could also be taken to work for D. H. Lawrence's position in society. At the time of writing the poem, he was living in voluntary exile. He left England in 1919 after the war years when both the reaction to his work and his marriage to a German divorcee were making it intolerable for them to stay. Among literary circles of the time, however, in Europe and America, he was recognized as a great writer.

EXPRESSING DUALITY

The symbolic act of renewal or rebirth is also found in the snake's ability to shed its old skin with a new one underneath. Over thirty years ago, I wrote a poem called *Snake;* I inhabited its voice. My female snake, however, did not slake off her outer skin but revealed an inner pattern of vulnerability which melded with the nature of her outer force. This poem for me represented the integration of vulnerability and power to express the merging of my outer and inner selves in my real mid-thirties.

Snake

my coat is tight   it is worn out
I need to swell my flesh   slough it off

this skin has served me well
I have had its use
now the inner pattern must reveal myself again

but in the heat her snake-skin smoulders
melds   submerges   inside out
the used   the vulnerable interfuses   interlocks
no slaking off   but fusion of her forces fresh

she hisses:
I cleave my power amidst the ancient-wise and each new day

and that is what I need to do
and all I need to do

(1983)

I wrote this poem so long ago I remember little of the circum-stances, but something in me had found a wise voice to articulate the fusing of the old and the new. And I kept it hand-written in my files. In order to have found that snake's voice, I must have inhabited its spirit and made contact with an ancient wisdom, tapping into the underlying power of the archetypal snake. I had found my own voice through the image of the snake shedding its outer skin.

Usually the wise voice speaks directly through me only after pages of scribble; then when it comes, it requires barely any re-writing. When I first wrote this poem I knew nothing of line-breaks to bring out the inherent meaning so I altered them later. I spaced out some of the words to emphasize the changing nature of the coat and emotional state. Italics indicate direct speech in the first, second and last stanza. There is only one punctuation mark in the whole poem: the colon which denotes a change of tone to that wise voice of the hiss.

The third stanza, however, is in the third person: both visual and conceptual. This allowed the poem's narrator to describe how the skin was not sloughed off but made for a merging of the snake's forces. Writing had brought awareness into my thirty-something self and led to renewal, as worn out layers were cast off and patterns of the inner self were revealed. It was a turning inside out, as outer and inner self fused in a new way.

THE OUROBOROS

The serpent biting its own tail
dates back to ancient Egypt and Greece.
The eternal cycle of life is just another of the implicit meanings

There are times when I sense a poem emerging and it feels like the words and voice come through me containing more than I ever thought I was going to write about. This is such a poem:

Ouroboros

Here is the golden snake on his way
along the bridge from eternity to now.

He comes from no beginning
He goes towards no end
When he rests he loops himself
until his mouth encloses his tail
and he sucks in time until it disappears

And there is no end and no beginning
And no separation of heaven from earth
When your eyes are open, watchful
for his sharp tongue, his sudden movement

As long as you know how to let your footsteps
tread along the bridge one foot after the other

(2006)

The poem came from a freewrite about time; I used the following sentence as a prompt:

I need a bridge between eternity and the present day

The snake is male. Why I choose one gender or the other for the snakes in my poems I have no idea. There is much about a poem I do not realize until after writing it. Particularly the ones which come more or less whole and need barely any redrafting. But I consider punctuation and layout only after I see the words on the page or screen. That is part of my redrafting process.

With *Ouborbos*, punctuation is minimal to emphasize the sense of continuity and flow with no full stop at the end. But a capital letter at the beginning of a new line gives a fresh thought. Only 'now' at the end of the first stanza has a full stop because the word gives the sense of the present moment in time. The third stanza has a couple of commas with one after 'sharp tongue', to create a pause and increase the idea of the 'sudden movement' afterwards. Otherwise no other marks between the words.

This poem called on the ancient image and was easy to read and I read it at many poetry events. That usually happens some time after the poem has settled down, and I become ready to read it in public or to others. Although reading to writing friends helps me tweak a poem when I hear it bounce back to my own ears outside the privacy of my own four walls, and listen to their feedback. I always read aloud to myself as I write to hear how words sound whether prose or a poem. But curiously the spoken poem often sounds different, depending on the audience or individual listener.

I remember being astonished in the first week of the MA Course at Sussex, when our tutors stood up to read to all the new students. I remember thinking, I could never do that. One year later, there I was standing up reading to tutors and students alike. And now fifteen years on, the thought of standing up and reading, and relating to an audience excites me. It makes me feel alive as the writing makes me aware of the energetic flow from brain, heart and flesh down to my fingers and out connecting to the world. It is visceral in its nature. It completes another kind of circle, finishes the loop of voice to myself, then to people as an audience, and not only to them but back to me yet again in their presence. So different from reading aloud and alone at home.

When I read *Ouroboros*, I visualized the golden snake. When I said 'you' I meant myself, and anyone in the audience. It was as if in addressing them as well, they too needed to be watchful for the 'sudden movement', know how to put 'one foot after the other' as we all do in life. That is often how we perceive time in a linear fashion and yet the image of the snake's body is in a circular loop. And that makes time continuous. The symbol for eternity.

SNAKESKIN

Note-Book Spain 2004

I found the snake-skin on the side of the road: it was pretty with grey and silver markings. I brought it home without damaging the precious surface. It was beautiful and fragile. But we have a taboo in our family around snakes: nothing is allowed in the house about them. Not an image, not even the word and certainly not the real thing. I could not keep it on display in the house at all. I thought if I can't keep it, I'll burn it and lit a fire. As I was about to drop it in, my hand literally would not let me carry this out. It refused. I hid the snakeskin out of sight of the family.

Not long after, I was sitting in an aisle of Rochester Cathedral one autumn afternoon as my then-husband and daughter were in a long rehearsal for 'The Armed Man' by Karl Jenkins. I had planned to listen and do some writing. The following poem was written that afternoon.

SnakeSkin

Here – I give you this snake-skin
it's yours – later I will tell you the story
how I picked it up off the road-side.

Here – coil it loosely in your palm –
keep it hidden in some secret drawer.

Wear this sloughed off thing when you feel temptation
pulling – preen yourself in its silver grey markings;
this beauty will not startle; all venom is spent.

Look through these lidless slits where once eyes peered
furrow the earth with your belly
                    follow the trail to unknown places.

But what if it is a creeping thing I give you
beyond a simple gift, what if in its skin
                    are residues of sinister intent.
If so, we will burn it.

I also read this poem at several poetry events over one summer. Again as with *Ouroboros*, I made a connection with the audience. Reading sped up in the middle stanzas and then slowed down again for the last. My voice felt confident as I imagined I was giving the snakeskin to each person.

In our western culture we meet the snake as a malevolent serpent in the Garden of Eden at the beginning of the Bible (Genesis 3:1-15). God condemned the creature to slither in the dust after tempting Eve to eat the fruit from the forbidden tree of good and evil. The snake's reptilian body gives rise to so many different stories. As well as being lethal with its sting, and healing if venom is used medicinally.*

The undertones of *SnakeSkin* dealt with this duality endemic in the snake's body, although it was about the skin and not the creature within. The significance here lay in the snakeskin being a gift of beauty, but with the heightened awareness that if there were any 'residues' of poison left, both giver and receiver would burn it together.

Some time later I gave the original snakeskin to a friend who I knew would value it as I could not keep it myself. *SnakeSkin* as poem and thing then became a real gift.

BLISS of BEING

Sensations of light or gold
travelling in waves through my body
gentle pulsation through my flesh
a sense of bliss in my being
a oneness with the invisible universe of which I am part
(2012)

A few lines captured this fleeting moment. Pleasurable to read back later. I experienced this during a treatment with my cranial osteopath. He talked about the still point* at the centre of the physiological body connecting with the wider world energy. This bliss originated from the solar plexus chakra.* A feeling in the core of my being; one of pure energy pulsating through me giving me the intense physical pleasure of being an alive being, being *alert* to my own aliveness. The writing was lyrical to match the sensations.

Then a memory surfaced from my training course in Biodynamic Psychotherapy in the seventies (this was developed by Gerda Boyesen*). She spoke of *streamings*: I identified the wonderful sensations I had experienced as this energetic flow. Boyesen's theory explained that under the emotional and physiological stress held in body and mind lies a suppressed and potential energy like an electrical current. She compared this to the flow of an oceanic wave; a life-force in waiting which would give a sense of 'well-being, feelings of pleasure and security' (Boyesen 1976, pp. 81-98).

LIFE FORCE ENERGY

This chapter having set out with one theme in mind, the process and energy of writing led elsewhere and I thought at times had distracted me into those stories about the snake. I had plenty more I left out. And reluctantly. There are so many. Starting with the theme of *erotic alert* I was drawn into the wily ways of the snake's energy and its complexity as the snake slithered through the poems, prose and stories.

I followed that lead enjoyably. Even though this definitely felt like a wandering around my writings. The writing, however, held onto duality as a constant: masculine and feminine, Lawrence's education and instincts, grown-up and naïve voices, inner and outer selves, time and infinity, poison and healing. With the force of the underlying theme of opposites implicit in androgyny as an archetype, it had its own underlying power to influence the trajectory of the writing. No surprise on reflection, but not obvious during the writing process. Insights so often only come after the writing is done and finally edited.

I followed the writing which had its own intelligence and integrity and this chapter after all then developed its own coherence. Ending as it did on the deeper force of my fundamental life energy. Writing about *erotic alert* took me into a different reality than the one I thought it might. My reality is what I care about. A reality outside the Garden of Eden, where neither Adam and Eve, nor any of us live.

My reality in the next chapter is revealed through the uncovering of my heart – ripped apart, but never broken.

Writing To Do

Scribble & Flow
Follow-the-flow-of-your-mind, the key to all writing

Begin every session by writing for six minutes with no given subject. Allow the hand to follow the flow of whatever appears on the page: you will find subjects to write about appear on their own: if they don't, then describe something about your surroundings, or that you feel.

Gillie Bolton (2014)

In the *Writer's Key* this is how Gillie Bolton suggests every writing session could usefully begin. It's a limbering up before tackling specific exercises.

Scribble freely – keep going with the words that come without thinking too much what sense is being made. All the technical skills of writing: redrafting, adding punctuation, editing can come later. Maybe you will craft this writing, maybe you will scrunch it up and chuck. It is practice. Well worth doing.

Ambivalence
Focus on a conflict
One where your head and instincts are at odds with each other

- Write from the perspective of your head
- Write from the perspective of your instincts eg: from heart or guts
- Write again expanding with more detail

- Change your perspective by taking on the 'I' Voice of each
- Write a dialogue between these two Voices
- Keep writing until you reach some sort of resolution

- Write again about your conflict
- Write about how you feel about it now
- If you haven't resolved your ambivalence, let it rest for now

You'll probably want to spread this writing over a number of days

Writing To Do

Symbol ♂ ♀

Something representing another thing like images for male and female
Something used to represent an idea or quality

Metaphor

Ouroboros: the circle of the snake
is a metaphor for eternity
One solid thing to describe an abstract thing or feeling

Archetype

Archetypes are pure essential qualities
manifested differently according to a particular age
Botticelli's Primavera or Michelangelo's David
represent Renaissance female and male archetypes

Enjoy a scribble and freewrite (ignore grammar, spelling, punctuation)

- Describe the clothes or watch you wear as a symbol of your gender
- Describe something you own that might be a symbol of your opposite gender inner self
- Describe a creature of the land, sea or sky which is a metaphor for how you feel about your gender
- Describe a creature of the land, sea or sky which is a metaphor of your inner self of the opposite gender
- Describe the qualities that come to mind when you think of a female archetype
- Describe the qualities that come to mind when you think of a male archetype
- Using what you have learnt from the above exercises, write a reflective piece about yourself at the present time, referring to your age and gender

Psychotherapy and Writing

Some of the ways of writing in this book have been influenced by my training in humanistic psychotherapies during the seventies: particularly dramatic dialogues and dream writing which are rooted in my experience of Gestalt Therapy. Humanistic psychotherapies evolved in the mid-twentieth century out of the psychoanalytic movement. The underlying principle supports the individual to make choices to become a healthy and fulfilled person placing the authority with the individual, rather than the expert practitioner whose role is to guide and understand. *Writing for Wellbeing* extends this potential through creative exploration.

Carl Jung's Contribution to our Language

Many Jungian words have been taken up in our everyday speech. In this chapter I have drawn on the *animus* and the *anima*. The *archetypal* nature of the snake in D.H.Lawrence's long narrative poem showed his *shadow** personality in the clumsy throwing of the stick at the disappearing snake.

*Synchronicity** rather than co-incidence is another of Jung's words when seemingly unrelated events connect themselves. Sometimes this occurs in uncanny ways with writing, which remains private, but alters circumstances in the outside world. How we all might tap into a vast invisible and unknowable world, Jung called the *collective unconscious.**

Freewriting & the Unconscious

Freewriting* is a technique of allowing writing to flow in a stream with whatever content comes into your mind without any rules at all. Sometimes memories will float up from the past. Different perspectives and understanding may find expression. Links may be made that hadn't occurred to you. This is writing without self-criticism or judgement. It's a wonderful way of freeing yourself up and can form the foundation of your writing, long before the need to redraft and edit.

Freud asked his patients to *free associate** from their dreams as he sat behind them; they were lying on a couch and would not be distracted by seeing him. He used this as a starting point to explore their unconscious thoughts and neurosis (Jung 1964, p. 27). Freud's *royal road to the unconscious* led to his interpretations of dreams.

Apparently Freud was influenced by an author: Ludwig Börne (1786–1837) who wrote an essay: *The Art Of Becoming an Original Writer in Three Days* (1823) about writing down 'everything that comes into your head' (Jones 1967, p. 219). Freewriting clearly has its roots far earlier than we might have imagined. Given time and opportunity the unconscious obliges and lets things pop into the mind, allowing inhibitions to dissolve. Virginia Woolf used a similar idea with the stream of consciousness. *Writing Without a Parachute: The Art of Freefall* by Barbara Turner-Vesselago is a contemporary book showing the value of surrendering to the creative process of writing.

CHAPTER 3

Raw Heart

Let Him Kiss Me with the Kisses of His Mouth
The Song of Solomon (i:ii)

Let me kiss you with the kisses of my mouth is how I might rewrite this first line for the Queen of Sheba, for her love. Both ways of writing are evocative and rather wonderful. I feel daring when I rewrite famous lines, but once done it is tempting to think I might just do it again. It is only playing with words. I like that line both ways.

This is far from a playful chapter; here I examine how I explore in writing a raw and hurt heart when kisses are lost. I have left behind the energy which infused my writing in the last chapter, and the blissful experience of my core life-force, as I deal with separation when love, with and for another, is lost and pain enters the heart.

With the benefit of a long life, I am able to draw on writing which goes back many years as I deal with two vital relationships: a lover, and a husband. In the middle of the chapter the artist Edvard Munch appears. Why have I allowed him into this book? A major exhibition* of his work in London coincided with tensions in my marriage: sitting in the galleries reflecting on his art and my own life, proved an excellent stimulus for expressing and delving into my own dilemmas through writing.

But I start with the loss of a lover from what feels like another lifetime, many years ago. The writing, however, still means a lot to me because in another sense Love is timeless, and this relationship stays inside me almost bubble-wrapped with my poems and prose.

THE END OF A LOVE STORY

Endings are common enough. Here is the briefest of explanations to an ending as if starting a story. I have used the simplest of words, language I find helpful when writing about the adult nature of relationships.

Once upon a time quite a long time ago there were two people. The next day one of those two people walked away in the opposite direction, took a plane to the other side of the world.

I put my grown-up feelings into two long poems which I kept hand-written; I read them every few years for many years. These few lines belonged to one of them:

there is the heart
folded around, tight
as a walnut and cold

That metaphor of the walnut with its convoluted folds rather like a brain worked well for this love. My heart certainly chilled but it was never broken; it proved to be too resilient. Maybe all those folds kept my heart safe and the metaphor was apt.

Years and years later, one night around midnight, I dared myself to do a Google search for the lover, long gone. Here is my poem:

Finding You

It was an idle moment
                  late into the evening.
I was sitting in front of my computer: flat screen
world wide web whirring   Google box cleared: for Search

Breath held
I type in your name   Quick   Easy
With my middle finger I lightly touch   *Enter*

There you are:
entire web sites with your familiar name
listed, shared with others eminent in your field.
I highlight one   press the mouse   *Enter further*

In front of my eyes:
your expertise evaluated, linked into professional circles.
Your work profile   Contact details   Tempting
No. This poem will suffice.

It is years since we whispered our names
in sunlit rooms with curtains closed,
in the wilds of Hampstead Heath
and Hadley Woods.

Into the double helix of my being, your name is seared
I know where you are.

The ambiguity of the poem, daring to find her on the web, but discovering through the unfolding of the writing, that something of her was also found in me. Articulated like that. That was pretty powerful. Made me feel closer. Alone. True. Yet feeling connected through writing the poem. And accepting I was absolutely and irreconcilably separated from someone loved. But my inner life had been infused with a deeper knowledge of passion for a real live breathing person, albeit a temporary presence in my life. The essence of the passion in the end overrode the pain of separation and remained.

As always the writing stepped in, gave me the freedom to express whatever I needed to say, however I wanted to say it and however many years later. I had a great deal to say and wrote it all down: love, anger, fury . . . the lot, as well as gratitude for experiencing that kind of reciprocal love.

GOODBYE KISSES

Then quite unexpectedly many years later, my heart started to wake up once again. I wanted, needed, and was able to let go of that relationship a little more. I did so with another poem:

Good-Bye Kisses

It was kisses, I stashed away
in that secret drawer, then hid the key
only for me to find.

I filed in all the quickly snatched ones,
tight up against each other, then I stacked those lips
picked up from long grasses, slid off shafts of sunlight
and yes, no forgetting that hard snog pressed into tree bark.

I'm sifting kiss after kiss from first to last
transferring them into a box with a close-fitting lid.

All but one piled in – no fuss.
Not so the kiss upfront
Out it slips – still thrills

me – lying on the sofa   pulling you down
the restless playing of a Mozart piano concerto
your burnished hair   the never ending cadenza

Certainly that one will go in
none of them will fray or fade
I'll peep inside whenever I want.

My secret drawer – that's cleared now
lined with something blue
The new key is in my hands.

That poem released feelings about memories, placing them more firmly into the past. I chose kisses as memorable and sometimes, I think, even more intimate than sex. That amazing implosion of sensitivity in the lips, and then tongue, alerting the body further down for more.

Writing my poems and scribbling many more freewrites was valuable as part of the unravelling of my emotional history. Writing kept me grounded and helped to make sense of my life. I did not share these writings with anyone, but the poems arose out of all that scrawling. Eventually, however, I shared the poems. That process was part of the letting go.

It was painful because what had felt so private became public in the poems. But writing and reading to others (at first only to those close to me) allowed for owning my deep internal processing without revealing any of the detailed knowledge about the relationship. With hindsight it probably took me around twenty-five years to feel no visceral pangs at all. Such a relationship had become part of my body: physical, mental, spiritual. Writing embodied an externalized form outside of myself which helped assimilate the obvious separation which had taken place so much earlier in real life.

Why did I choose kisses for the poem? When I started writing, the memories of kisses in different places came to me and I wanted to write about them. I did the writing as if the *kisses* chose me. Only later did it become apparent why I would choose kisses rather than sex itself. Kisses are good. Sex is difficult to write about. And in missing love-making, it was the kisses I wanted to preserve in a poem. Not sex. Nor any other memory.

THE SECRET DRAWER

There was a real secret drawer – it belonged to my grandmother's French cabinet with a rose pink marble top and veneered panels decorated intricately with flowers and curlicues to the front and sides. I was very fond of it and loved its secret drawer that opened when I searched inside for an indentation to press with my finger which released the drawer.

It worked well as a metaphor for an awakening heart. I had another metaphor too for the future: *a new key* and the drawer cleared and *lined with something blue*. Meanwhile, new heart energy took me into a different place in my life.

What I didn't know was that my heart, which had been startled into new feelings of love, was beginning to unfold once more. Revealed itself raw, felt ripped apart. That is what I wrote about next:

        my heart   shaved

a cross-section   four chambers

open   pulsing

                         four chambers pulsing

raw red   shaved

               pared apart

                           revealing

Sliced and cleft

          revealing

             a whole life   reaching out

blood flowing to hands   holding tight   forced

off   fingers holding tight   forced

                       off

                       navigating

   others

Scary feelings. Scary writing. Shaving a section of heart at the beginning, as if to be seen surgically; the repetitive phrases picking up from each other with white space between, and the layout and sparseness of the language packs in the feelings. When read aloud the prose-poem gathers momentum and speed, even with the pauses in those spaces. And ends with all that *reaching out, holding tight* and finally *forced off* in the business of *navigating others*. A mainly nautical word implying a boat in danger at sea with the desperation of holding on until that last word *others* falls away in inflection and resignation.

The poem's power lies in the layout with no punctuation. In contrast to the content, I have had a bit of fun with the following block of punctuation marks. I did not need them, but here they are in just in case . . .

PUNCTUATION IF NEEDED*

,,

.,.

.,.

;;;;;;;;;;;;;;;;;;;;;;;;;;;;;;;;;;;

!?!?!?!?!?!?!?!?!?!?!?!?!?!?!

. . . .!!!. . . . .

()()()()()()()()()()()()()()()()(

WORDS ONLY

my heart shaved a cross-section four chambers open pulsing four chambers pulsing raw red shaved pared apart revealing Sliced and cleft revealing a whole life reaching out blood flowing to hands holding tight forced off fingers holding tight forced off navigating others

Love & Loss

EDVARD MUNCH

Writing about my own heart coincided with visits to an art exhibition in London of Munch's self-portraits. As a Friend of the Royal Academy and able to visit as often as I liked, I kept wanting to return for more looking, more careful observation and more reflection. I was drawn back to look at the works of art in great detail; I scribbled away sitting on the comfortable benches in the middle of the gallery. It gave me time away from home to reflect on the buried pain in my heart that had surfaced and was unfamiliar.

When I take out my notebook at an exhibition, I have already walked through all the galleries, noting what jumps out at me and beckons me to linger and look. I may avoid the headphones giving me an audio guide, but I will skim the information displayed for names, titles and dates. My A5 notebook from the Munch Exhibition (2005) is fawn coloured, full of scribbled snatches which ignore the horizontal lines – lots of dates, titles, sketches with colours indicated:

> brown splodges, red lips, mauves, greens, dribbles of blue – canvas showing through. Drypoint on copperplate.
> Oslo. 1902: hand shot.
> 03/11/05 Munch 3rd Visit . . . I do not connect with him.

I went through all my jottings from these visits and later developed writing from the notes:

> Munch. Unattractive. A man from whom I would only walk away. But not from his paintings which I admire.

Munch was a fine artist, etcher and print-maker, often portraying his inner life onto canvas. He could only handle commitment to his art, not to lovers. He failed disastrously, if not tragically, in love and put all of that into dark and sinister paintings.

As I wrote in the gallery, I addressed Munch directly as if he was there through his own painterly representation of himself. I chose one in particular *Self Portrait in Light Coat with Yellow Background,* painted in 1915:

I would not let you touch me. I would rather be alone than have a cup of tea with you Munch. You wring pain from your heart into paint onto canvas. Careful compositions of dripping splodges. I would walk away from you. Maybe that is my own projected feelings* of your own walking away from women.

My main question about you Munch is: *does your art please my eye? How does it make me write?* Your subject matter makes me think of disconnection, particularly with the stories and series of paintings about the tragic aftermath of your relationship with Tulla Larsen,* when your left hand was shattered with a bullet (Prideaux 2005, pp. 221-225).

When I was back home, I started to type directly onto the screen in sea-green lettering which unfortunately I cannot show with black print on a white surface. I used the third person pronoun:

Her heart feels large, red, raw. Like a lump of meat inside the rib cage cut open. She has woken up twice with her heart raw like ripped flesh. She has never had such a feeling ever before. Once she wrote of her heart *tight as a walnut and cold.* This is the opposite.

I often write with colour because it imparts a different feeling. Reading this back to myself I have no idea why I did not use red to mirror the red heart but traditionally green is reminiscent of spring, new shoots in the garden, renewal, rebirth. I engaged with the sea-green lettering's own 'I' Voice and kept myself in the third person:

> I am this sea-green colour. I am soothing in tone. I ease the pain in her heart with my gentle colour, contain the shapes of the letters I form directly onto her screen.

This was a time when I had a very busy family life and felt receptive to all the different loves in my everyday life. My heart was awakening and yet with that came old, dormant hurts. Separation from the person loved or from the experience of a total love does rip the heart apart, leave it raw, however much in the past. But these images were concealed as I felt new waves of a different loving energy enter my heart. And then the rawness let itself be known. And I wrote to contain the distress.

A month later I had a more straightforward write, straight onto the screen again: *Heart Poem*. There are no scribbles in my file. It was a very neat uncomplicated piece of writing: gentle, unthreatening. About another waking up in the middle of the night, needing to go back to sleep, ready for an early morning start. In my diary, I wrote:

> My heart feels hidden; all images are feint. Lying here is empty of comfort. I am in a strange neutrality: alive but not feeling vibrant.

By using the spelling *feint* rather than faint, I meant the implicit lightness of a line on paper and by inference my heart; not the implication of weakness. With the ever faithful cup of tea, I comforted myself as I often did.

Heart Poem

Peel back flesh from the chambers of her heart
like a doll's house all neatly furnished
with miniature people fitted into living rooms
echoing the smallness of reality.

She lies underneath two duvets
in bitter cold night, in silent room,
in the inside darkness of small hours
in dressing gown she pads downstairs

makes mug of tea, strokes the cat
does not turn on hall light
to tread upstairs – she likes
the sweet liquid heat spreading
as sleep returns and her heart folds up.

CONVERSATION WITH MUNCH

I felt the great Scream in Nature
Inscribed in Munch's own hand on the frame of *The Scream**

Each time I was drawn back to the Munch exhibition, I focussed
on different paintings. I felt I was beginning to make some kind of
relationship, and started to address him by his first name:

Edvard
your hand has painted onto canvas the static sound of pain
moving through this world, through all our worlds.

Yes, Munch
the whole world knows about your pain, your scream.
The silent scream of the heart's pain
for the world, and for oneself.

This has become such an iconic image for the twentieth century. *The Scream* echoes through the universality of pain in the world and the individual so we may think of a more personal scream:

The sadness in her eyes reflect the tears which always come
and the silent scream of loss

Born in 1863, Munch lived through the horrors of two world wars. And as a child he experienced his own losses. At five years old his mother died, and as he emerged into adolescence his closest sister, Sophie, died.

When I wrote in the gallery I went through different stages: the first was careful observation of the painting, looking at content, style, line, colour, texture, composition. Then I followed with my own emotional response, and explored that. I asked myself various simple questions, finding this *abc* approach helpful. What was I feeling when I looked at the painting? How did I respond to those feelings? What was being triggered within me? I scribbled everything down.

Munch captured the stage of romantic love beautifully. *Attraction** shows a man and a woman merged in one outline of body, their cheeks touching. But the man is looking down, the woman looking up. There is no meeting of eyes. It prompted me to write the following:

I take this to be autobiographical, Edvard. The man looks at one with this woman. If it is indeed you: is this as close as you can get with cheeks touching? That soft touch of a lover's cheek. Is that the place on your cheek, a dry point where once your Mother's lips softly kissed her boy, caressed you with a light touch?

In all his relationships with women separation was the end game. His love life was a disaster. It is easy to reflect on the impact of losing his mother and sister so early in his life. My own looking at the Munch paintings allowed me to pivot back into my own life, stimulated the writings about feeling separate, as well as the explicit writings about the raw heart. It all became intermingled, and then I disentangled them. Made the writings stand alone.

MY MARRIAGE AND MUNCH WRITINGS

Yesterday evening I sat in front of the fire and read the writings to my husband. The Munch exploration is the peg I am giving these writings. These are my interiority. A place inside I can barely articulate. At times a wordless place from pre-verbal existence. My own intense, on-going and never-letting up journey. So completely self-involving, I barely have a handle on my life.

I do not remember if it was the same evening, or a few evenings later. Probably it was later in the week as reading to my husband usually made us closer; he told me he liked the writing. Yet he also added not long afterwards: *how difficult it is living with you who have such intense inner experiences*.

What follows is a continuation of the same story. I swapped around with my pronouns in the narrative. My husband became an impersonal *he*. I did not name him. That is how it was in the writing at the time. I was not avoiding naming him. I called him *he* because I wanted to neutralize the upsetting effect he was having on me. The third person pronoun is useful for that sort of reason.

As I addressed myself, at times I used the first person pronoun, then switched to the second person 'you'. This was an attempt to make connection with myself through a few words of permissive comfort. This was a 'me' I too found difficult to live with, let alone him. I had no choice. I felt disconnected from myself, kept going with routine necessary tasks:

> There is food in the house and food on the table. This is what brings us together each day, shared eating of our food. Our most basic nourishment we all enjoy without question. My hands sweep the floor, empty the rubbish bin, wipe the table clean for supper. I say to myself: *you are allowed to disconnect. You can do these small tasks*. And this permission thaws out the chill, connects head to heart.

Our own connection was not good. Not good at all. There was discord in the marriage, which I explored and expressed in my writing.

> The time between us is frosted over, glazed with accusations. His temper distances me, strengthens over the washing up. Eventually I said: *I have no response. I cannot use words any longer.*

I took myself off to my workroom. Here I knew I would find the words. The ones in the paragraphs which follow. A vivid memory, even more so because I captured the moment as it happened:

> Connected to writing now. Yes. Left off with pencil on paper. Heart warms as I type direct onto screen. Too much writing at the end of my fast fingers. He walks in and I tell him:
>
> *I am near tears trying to write this.*
> *Oh love*, he says, *you are in a state.*

∞

I am at the heart of myself
I have never ever felt so vulnerable with awareness
This is the experience of the exposed heart
and I cannot protect myself.
I am in such a raw place beyond anger.

Our separateness from each other becomes even more obvious in the next piece. I distanced both of us further by calling us the man, the woman. We could be any husband and wife closing the door after a bad evening.

On Closing The Door

He allows hate into the evening; I go to my room, shut the door.
I do not like a closed door. I go to my room, shut the door.
Turn the light off.

∞

The man says:

It was good when you went to your room, when you closed your door. I realized my separation; I knew I did not have to make you see the world the way I see it. I stopped needing to reach you. My feelings settled within myself, separate from you. The closed door broke our connection.

∞

The woman lies in bed in her own isolation, pillows plumped up behind her head, duvet soft, snug around her body. Curtains drawn like two flags across the black iron rod.

The centre of her heart has a pin-prick hole. She feels barely in her own life. There are no images of comfort. There are no thoughts of comfort. There are no feelings of comfort. In this raw place there is only one question repeating itself over and over: *Why is it like this?*

The man continues:

Later I opened your door, you were asleep in your bed which is ours but which I only come into occasionally. I opened your door after I'd upset you earlier in the evening and said: *sorry* . . . as you lay asleep, and then I closed the door quietly and told you in the morning.

∞

A few years later there was a proper separation, an amicable parting between my husband and myself. Nevertheless there were painful months, if not several years, whilst we carried on writing to each other with emails and we found that really effective and helpful. We were able to articulate ourselves at a distance from each other when our meetings were razor sharp. We wrote thoughtfully to each other and our underlying friendship eventually was able to emerge and sustain us.

CORRESPONDENCE WITH MY HEART

After our separation, I travelled to the Moroccan desert and wrote these 'heart' letters. My heart had come home, I felt at last, when I discovered the desert in my sixties. Here I arrived at a restful place: yellow sand dunes, blue skies. The kind of Abyssinian desert* Sheba might have crossed on her journey home from Solomon's Palace in Jerusalem (Briggs 2005, p. 22).

The rhiyad (guest house) was reached along ancient tracks into the desert proper, and near a huddle of Berber dwellings. I stayed for a week. Here I was given one room in the corner of a spacious, rectangular walled compound where I could write, make tea and sleep. In the sandy soil young trees of fig, orange, eucalyptus and almond had been planted to provide shade and shelter.

The Unsent Letter is one of my favourite strategies for exploratory writing. I find it brilliant for expressing the unspoken to people with whom I might not have an open and honest rapport. Helpful to see what I want to say and then write their imagined replies back to myself. I do this a lot in my diary; it helps with insights as well as letting go of annoying and nagging feelings.

Letter writing I find is also effective for parts of myself as well as other inanimate objects. Here I have a two-way correspondence with my own heart, starting with a letter from my heart:

Dear Monica,

There is only one of me to each body and one just for you. I have feelings: gentle ones which suffuse along and down your arms into hands which reach out. At times I close off, but mostly I'm ready to spread the love outwards.

Connections. Mine. Many. Sometimes fleeting. Also committed. That's what I do. I can tell you about heart connections. I can tell you about intimacy. But no one heart beating against your own. Separated only by skin, flesh and blood.

lots of loving,

your heart

Dear Heart,

You think you may tell me about intimacy. For my 63 years I have little to show: not much on the outside has changed. I still have those gentle feelings reaching out. I am still able to touch those fiery feelings that know they may as well not reach out, and shrink back in resignation.

Tell me: *Are you still a bit raw? A bit ragged?* You like to tell me all about the gentle love: *but what about my lonely self?*

Let me tell you: *do you know how lonely I am?* I feel you whole and big. I feel you securely there behind my ribs. I know you are there. I know you have a lot to give. There is, I know, a healing of the rawness. There is a softening of the ruggedness.

Let me tell you this: you make me angry. Giving and giving. Receiving, yes. But essentially you are an alone heart. On your own terms. No compromise. Alone. Full. And prepared to be alone. *What have you to say about my loneliness? Your rawness? Is it really gone?*

Yours sincerely,

Monica

Dear Monica,

I am no longer raw. I am not ragged. I am here – always here for you. Loving you first. Loving others. Varying loves. Lots of loving. That's what I do best.

Don't you *sincerely* me. I send you love always. I do not let you down. I keep you happy. You have nothing to complain of. *With me inside you how can you feel lonely?*

Please explain.

love,

your heart xxx

Dear Heart,

This is the intimate me. Not intimacy with another. Isn't that what I want? That is what I appear to have sought all my life and failed. *Haven't you let me down?* With this huge need that I continually have to adjust to doing without.

It's all very well being alone, and liking it. But it's not actually, not 24/7 enjoyable. No. So I feel you've given me great expectations of intimacy and it's all come to nothing. I like being alone. I also like to seek closeness. There you sit inside me suffusing to the world. Giving to me. And I have to be my own rock.

Yours,

Monica

Dear Monica,

Your own rock. Well that's good surely. Anyway your life is not over yet. You have loved and lost and not been fearful about loving again. That is good. You have been brave about love. Your story continues. Your heart is much healed. I have no answer. You go forward well, whole, and open-minded. Lonely and not so lonely. We'll review your situation in the years to come. That has to be enough for now.

xx heart love

That interchange made me realize that my story was not over yet. Wise words from within me. That Wise Voice I find in my writing. Ever hopeful. Ever optimistic. The concept of being my own rock came surprisingly after feeling angry. By the end of this *exploratory and expressive* writing, I felt a surge of receptivity to life opening up in my heart and optimism for the future.

My Moroccan stay in a place away from it all was great for providing a perfect environment to write and reflect on love and matters of my heart.

It is true, my heart sits full, comfortable in my rib-cage. Deep inside the blood flows through me. This is where I feel at home. In the desert. Responding to the day. Perhaps thousands of years ago, my Hebrew ancestors were nomads in another desert. It is not so unlikely. I come home to my heart in the desert. Content. Perfectly safe.

The next chapter is about the writing which helped my heart
unfold as it was challenged and shocked unexpectedly into a new
kind of Loving.

Writing To Do

The Unsent Letter

A memory from forty years ago floated into my writing one day. I then set about an imaginary correspondence with the person in question. I did it for the sake of my writing but I did so reluctantly. There was no way I would have sent her a letter. Anyway I did not know where she lived, or if she was alive or dead. And I did not care. Writing to her made me uncomfortable, which confirmed an emotional charge had remained hidden all these years and was surfacing as I wrote.

Write an Unsent Letter to:

♦ a long lost lover
♦ your heart
♦ your anger
♦ your pain
♦ your sadness
♦ your regrets
♦ Love

Write replies, carry on with your correspondence until you reach a natural conclusion and a resolution is reached. Say what you really mean and have never said before.

Memory

I know my red hot anger. I knew my fury with my 28 year old self
What did I do when I was 28?
I walked into her room wearing black leather gloves
I took the photograph of me off her noticeboard
I tore it in two and left the pieces on her bed

I deliberately kept brief the unsent letters and replies back and forth. I gave the woman her own 'I' Voice to address me. This is what she wrote in the last reply (with my own hand of course):

You need never see me. We will not meet again.

And that was that. Despite not having seen her for decades, and unlikely to ever again, the writing was still curiously satisfying. It rounded off business I didn't realize was unfinished and buried from years and years ago.

Guidelines for Unsent Letters

If tempted to send, only do so if you are confident your letter will be received well. You might consider redrafting first.

Writing To Do

Ekphrastic writing: a vivid description
Most often a poem in response to a work of art.*

Suggestions for how to write about a painting:

In The Art Gallery

♦ Choose and focus on one particular painting
♦ Look closely and write a purely visual description at first

Ask yourself these questions:

♦ Have I missed anything?
♦ How is the painting framed?
♦ Can I identify the materials used?
♦ How does the size of the work sit on the wall where it is hung?

Describe more about the:

♦ Style
♦ Effect the artist has created
♦ Composition, lines, texture
♦ Colours and how they work with each other

Then turn your attention inwards:

♦ What are you feeling?
♦ How do you respond to those feelings?
♦ Is there anything in your own life that this connects to or is
  triggered?

Scribble everything down as it comes. Write down the name of the
painting, the artist, anything that catches your eye from the plaque on
the wall or information given. When you are at home perhaps do some
research into the artist, the time period, what experts have written. Write
more. And write more. Until you sense something emerging from your
writing, which you can play with and develop. Give yourself time. Weeks
or months. It doesn't have to come immediately.

Writing NOT TO DO

There are *Keep Out* areas when tackling creative therapeutic writing.

Listen and stop if you have a small inner voice saying:

♦ I don't want to do this writing

♦ I ought to do this writing

♦ I really feel resistant to do this writing

♦ I am ambivalent and uncertain about this writing

Ask yourself whether you have an obligation to write. Make a note perhaps for another time and put the writing to one side. But it can sometimes be helpful to find out why you don't want to write, or what it is you don't want to write about.

Start a sentence with one of these phrases:

♦ I don't want to write about . . . .

♦ I do not have to write because . . . .

♦ I'd rather do . . . .

Lay Out

White space is the writer's medium as much as the black lines of language.

Betsy Warland (2010)

Space on the Page

It's not only the words which matter when you place them on page or screen. The white space around your text, between your phrases, separating your lines are all like breaths and pauses in speech. What is not there is as important as the meaning underlying the content. With this in mind, you may emphasize the rhythm and pattern of your words.

Ask yourself these questions:

♦ What idea do you want to get across in your writing?

♦ Would gaps between phrases or words add to this meaning?

♦ How might more or less space between lines work?

It's only after a final draft that I start to play around with how the words look on the page. My prose poem (p. 40.) uses a lot of white space to draw out the feeling of a heart *pared apart, sliced and cleft and revealing.* On the next page, I bunch the words together in a few lines and place a square shape of punctuation more or less in the middle of the page. It makes a point. Irony, perhaps. Or just fun which I can do once the feelings are no longer inside me.

Margins

This box uses justification on the left side. In the main body of the chapters, both right and left sides are evened out ie: both margins are justified. Sometimes I like to centre the phrase under a heading as I've done with the Lawrence lines (p. 21) or the quote above.

Fonts*

There are numerous fonts to choose from. On the screen you can also make choices with italics, bold or regular type. My poem *Snake* (p. 23) uses italic for the Voice and regular text for the Narrator. On screen or paper you can pick a colour to match your mood. A font with child-like handwriting is effective when typing with a *naïve* or *inner child's* voice.

In this book, there are three choices of font:

♦ Dakota (a handwriting script) for the chapter titles, headings in boxes and the book title.

♦ Sabon is the main text; it's a serif script. That means it has tiny curlicues to the up and down strokes. These help the eye glide across as you read.

♦ Frutiger is used in these boxes. A sans serif script with clean lines, no additional curves or marks added to the main body of the letter. Ideal for giving information.

Just My Type – A Book About Fonts by Simon Garfield is a wonderful read

CHAPTER 4

Butterfly

In this chapter there are two separate strands of writing and reflection: the unfolding layers of Love in a relationship which was like no other that I had experienced, and the role of mothering over three decades. Love in my older years came when the expectation of another romantic relationship was nowhere in sight: neither within my horizons standing on the earth, nor a twinkle in the sky. And I did not anticipate following a path of reciprocal involvement. Although as in all relationships, the future was not apparent in the beginning.

Yet quite by surprise Love arrived and shook me up into a whirlwind. Flung me in the air. When I landed I wrote and wrote, and wrote myself into quite a different kind of relationship. Writing revealed a pattern of loving I had never found before; words flowed and taught me so much more about the different voices of love. In my journals I explored these varied voices: *the wise, the naïve* and *the lyrical*.

Finally this writing led me into a more universal expansion of loving so that my life became richer. But this thread of writing starts, however, at the beginning of a completely new life: the birth of my daughter 30 years ago.

NEW LIFE, NEW LOVE

After my husband went home in the evening, I sat up for most of the night writing on the hospital table swung across the bed, whilst holding the baby in my arms.

> I sat up until five in the morning just holding and looking at you and writing. I remember the midwife saying: *look there's your baby's head.*
>
> I looked down and saw your head coming out of my body, so surreal. I made a mental count of your eyes, mouth and nose, all there – all the time I felt so mentally alert.
>
> *
>
> I just needed to sit up and hold you all night. It's now ten to nine and you are just almost five and a half hours old. An absolutely perfect little face, quite peaceful. Not interested in sucking. I saw you were a girl immediately, no-one else noticed. You are exquisite and ours.
>
> *   *   *
>
> They say everyone cries on the third day when the milk comes in. I just feel very soft and vulnerable. I'm besotted with you.

Getting used to my new baby was why I needed to write, as well as recording the birth as soon as I could. I wrote myself into the experience of becoming a mother; crossing that threshold. Although I remember the day like yesterday, there are details that I do not remember like this vignette:

> I spoke to my seven year old niece on the phone and she said: *Monnie, is it true the baby really doesn't have a name?*

Reading back now uncovers forgotten gems and takes me back in time. My writing in those hours during the night followed the moments of falling in love with my baby as it happened: her alert expressive face, her eyes looking into mine, her tiny fingers curled around one of my own. I marvelled that this is how we all come into the world, yet the experience felt miraculous.

LOVE & WRITING

Loving my daughter as she grew up through adolescence was such a contrast to the love I received growing up. My own constrained upbringing and the influence my mother and father had on my early adult life became more and more obvious to me. I was determined to undo the kind of conditional love I had experienced myself as a child, teenager and young adult in the way I related to my own daughter. In time when she found a loving relationship of her own in her twenties, I only found pleasure.

Adult relationships I know often reflect the mother-to-baby love of our childhood. Now that I am so distanced from my own early experience of love whilst continuing to evolve in my relationship as a mother to my grown-up daughter, I really understand in an experiential visceral way, what is recognized as John Bowlby's attachment theory.*

During the course of healthy development attachment behaviour leads to the development of affectional bonds or attachments, initially between child and parent and later between adult and adult.

(Bowlby 1980, p. 39)

What strikes me is that the ever present constancy of my own writing has mirrored a nurturing role. Making up for the absence of the maternal experience I lacked from the past. Almost as if writing has become a character present in my day-to-day life. Although derived from within me, the externalization of my writing has become a constant force of stability. As an adult who felt failed as a child growing up, I now feel that the process of writing over time, alongside relationships which have nurtured me, has contributed to my feeling of security.

AN UNEXPECTED LOVE

New Love in my older years which was not following a pattern of a close relationship, yet did not feel entirely unrequited, brought up a quandary: *what was I to do about my feelings? How was I to relate?* Here is writing questioning how to approach this new love:

Sweeping Leaves

The eight o'clock sun is warm on my shoulders as I sweep the path on three sides of our house. I sweep and scoop up the winter-curled oak leaves from underneath stones, the withered wisteria blooms which only last week were fresh in their pale mauve scents, bits of twigs, cut the nettles back.

I could sweep for the rest of my day, the rest of my life like the monks set to sweep whilst brains coil and recoil. I am sweeping and clearing all the days up to this one. They line up behind this morning ready and waiting to be swept – not away – not swept away – but here to be brushed down with all that has been.

Old loves too tightly entwined all prised off, fallen and tumbled through too many years. I have no idea how to do this new love; a love which asks for its own truth ever since it surprised itself into existence. Let it breathe lightly in its own expansive way and find its own form as each day speaks and I listen to its voice.

Becoming aware that Love could find its own form whilst I swept the leaves up from my garden path put me in mind of the zen monks set to sweep monastery gardens or clear the leaves in front of their huts. Done slowly, like many necessary daily tasks, it becomes an enspirited practice. And in a way, I knew from the writing that a love could be like meditation and followed from moment to moment, day to day. I was not in control, not in a position of power, I was a follower of an energy like leaves obeying the laws of gravity and falling from their trees. I had to obey the laws of love which the writing helped me discover more than I knew before.

THE NAÏVE VOICE

Nevertheless there was another voice which became a pressing need to express. My preferred term is the *naïve*, rather than the *inner child*, because the place that voice comes from within me has adult sensibilities without the measured expression of my grown-up self. My language and phrases were freer and uninhibited. For years I kept the writing private, just for myself. My experience with my own mother had left me with uncomfortable feelings about loving, as if it was almost a crime.

Falling in love is not a crime although when I was a girl at secondary school, I and my sister huddled in our bedrooms talking about the latest crush out of ear-shot of Mother. With an upbringing where Love for others (in hindsight) was taboo at home and certainly at boarding school where girls who were too friendly were separated.

It is not a crime to love. But loving again in my fifties brought up old feelings of shame which only became apparent when I got the words down in the piece on the following page. It starts in the third person and then graduates to the 'I' voice as the writing comes to a close and is fully owned:

And it is a terrible thing if you want to say: *I love you* and the words are stuck and do not come out of the throat and it is like a ball of sunlight in the heart. If you say nothing the ball stays there. But then it wants to get its rays out and put the words on them. And if you can't tell these words – the sunlight swirls around and can't get out and makes the person uncomfortable with a lot of heat. They think it is so wrong and shameful to love another person even though they carry the sunlight in their heart.

And if the words from the heart can't find a way out through the voice they go round and round in the head all day long and all night long. And it is very tiring with words going round and round in the head with no way out through the mouth. You want to tell the person you love that I love you is what you want to say and this is awful.

It is awful because you do not know if they will mind that you love them but probably they love you too but you do not know because until you speak words about it between you and the other person no-one knows anything. And the truth can only be found in the words and that is what is good about the words that they lead to the truth and that is why I like words. But when the words get so close to the heart it is very scary.

And it is both very wonderful and both very awful. And this is awful because I never want to love someone one more time in my life who I might need and love too much and they do not love me and they will not like me because I like them and will disappear because of it.

I want to stop the going round of words in my head. I want to speak the words and if I can do that then maybe the fire of the sun will not get stuck inside my body and want to make me explode and the sun will shine its rays in the sky where it belongs.

In exposing the shame I was able to admit this to myself which softened the feelings and returned me to my grown-up self. I could not, however, escape having to address another insistent voice: a two year old in an adult body. This was even younger than the *naïve voice*.

Dialogue

2 yr old: What I want I want and I want it now and for now and for always and immediately

Adult Self: You know the score. You can't have what you want.

2 yr old: I have grown-up wantings because I am inside you. How dare you fob me off. You pretend I don't exist. I do.

Adult Self: You're forgetting you're two and cannot have what grown-ups want. I know it's difficult. Wantings are not bad just not possible. It's good to have the wantings but I am here to protect us both from them.

2 yr old: It is because of you I can't have what I want.

Adult Self: Yes. Only partly true though, it might not do you any good to have what you want. And in the end I don't care about the sex. I want the cuddles.

2 yr old: I like cuddles, and kisses. That's what I want too.

This resolution both surprised and pleased me. It was good not to deny the feelings and allow myself to own complex and layered emotions fully in my writing. This process helped to transform my awareness into what felt fitting and appropriate in real life.

Writing about Love was a tremendous challenge. Although I committed words to paper I only shared the *naïve* writing with a few trusted readers, and for more than ten years I kept the pieces in my files. I am willing to see them in print because I believe the impact of the *naïve voice* has been transformative for my adult self. I dared to write from a place which was full of vulnerability and that vulnerability has now become part of the older, more robust me.

At this point as a reader it may be a good idea to have a look at the boxes at the end of this chapter to see how I went about accessing my child-like voices.

LOVE IS A GIFT

What follows are two separate pieces of writing from my journals, spaced five years apart:

I have found myself doing the love thing in my writing. And it is held in writing not in the body. It gives me trust in what real love means for me, shows me how it exists, not through owning it as my particular love belonging to me to give — though paradoxically of course it is mine — knowing it exists of its own accord. Love just is. Like God just is. And I am just as I am. And I love. And I am lucky to be able to love like this. And there is a secret; it is to want and not want all at the same time. This is a secret hard won. This is a very powerful thing to do. All my writing leads to this.

Then five years later another journal extract shows this particular love has proved itself enduring:

Love is a gift as writing is a gift. By this I understand that although I may love, and it is me who writes, I do not own either with the ego-driven aspect of myself. In the early days of writing, I enjoyed a pride in what I achieved on the page. It's not to say that this is no longer the case. I would be daft to deny this. I am merely more humble about a gift I feel I am able to use. A gift which helps me live my life.

Without Writing, I would be bereft. Without Love, I would be bereft. Maybe it was a jolly good thing I found myself falling in love again at some point in my fifties. And that love too has proved to be a gift.

The next piece worked like magic. Something about Love changed for me on a specific day because of this writing. One summer's day walking along the coastal path in Norfolk when the waters had crossed the salt marshes and mingled with the freshwater right up to the bank of sea defences.

Tortoiseshell Box

It is a small heart-shaped tortoiseshell box, dark honey browns, shaded with translucent patches. Look inside, there is love nestling gently; and interwoven into red stranded ribbons binding lid to base are cornflowers. I must not undo these ribbons, so how may I open the lid.

Perhaps today I do not, knowing that inside this exquisite delicate heart box the love is there. It needs no disturbing, it needs no exposing, it needs no gazing into, or peering inside.

I know it is gently resting filling the whole of the heart box. No need to burst out, to explode into fireworks, into song and dance. No. This love is quiet, inhabits its own heart shape, gives out its own pulses, rhythms, invisible rays and is settled here today. A tortoiseshell heart box threaded with scarlet ribbons and blue cornflowers where trust and faith are interwoven, and which I will not finger apart. Love rests undisturbed trusting and above all knowing. I know love is inside the tortoiseshell heart box; I do not need to examine it. I do not need to do anything with it. What I need to do with this love inside the heart box is to know it; to know it deeper and deeper as part of me, and part of not me. How it exists beyond and outside of my own heart. That is what I need to know.

In my mind, the tortoiseshell heart box became small enough to transform into a locket:

I wear the locket against my breast bone, close to my own heart and with each pace, with each taking in of blue sky, blue waters, greenness all around, and swallows darting low, I feel this love flowing, feeding me, making me feel as I've never felt before, never overwhelming me, gently bathing me in love.

I trust this love. I have faith in it although I don't know where it will lead me. It is teaching me how to feel love, to experience love as a feeling, to have respect for love as a state of being, and nothing need be done beyond the feeling of it, knowing love exists within and without of me.

I am not responsible for where it leads me. I am responsible how I follow it, how I handle it, how I hold trust, how I handle myself with care, with respect, with knowing this love I hold is precious, unseen, felt and it is more than mine. It is a gift and I wear it today in a tortoiseshell translucent summer heart-shaped locket around my neck. And no-one, but no-one can see it.

LOVE, SECURITY, WRITING

With this writing, I have embraced a mature feeling of Love and learnt its enduring meaning. My varied styles of exploratory writing have given me a sense of security with Love taking its central place in my life.

Both the *naïve (inner) child* and the *wise adult* have expressed themselves freely in my writing. These permissions gave me layers of feelings to peel one from the other. Not one taking more power than another. All have their equal place within me. None denied or dismissed as silly. None taken more seriously than another. And through the writing, I have undone the destructive force of shame that was lying in wait to trip me up.

Loving one more person one more time, and without rejection or criticism at any time, has had the paradoxical effect of making

Love far more available for everyone it seems. I am able to reach out lovingly far more easily; my capacity to love feels fuller and richer. And I have my writing which accompanies me in daily life to thank profusely for providing me with the security I need and value.

Love

The chrysalis hangs
over-winter by a silk thread on the branch
which spreads itself across the yellow-blaze-risen sky

It feeds from tiny arrows
shot from the deep secrets of the blood-red earth

It unfurls like a green veined leaf on a May morning
as the butterfly opens its darling wings

Monica Suswin

Writing To Do

Helpful Guidelines:

- ◆ Follow where your writing takes you
- ◆ Learn to judge the kind of writing which helps you
- ◆ Take responsibility for what is good to write about
- ◆ Give yourself permission to express and write what you need
- ◆ Take responsibility for what you choose to share
- ◆ Respect your own emotional limits
- ◆ Trust the process of writing
- ◆ Stop when the energy fizzles out
- ◆ Explore writing with other writers as peers
- ◆ Find support at critical times for your writing with a trusted confidential other

Writing To Do

Love is a gift as writing is a gift

- Describe Love as a gift
- Describe the outside of a box or container which holds Love
- Look inside and write
- Write about your trust (or lack . . .) of love
- Trace the path love has taken you

Writing To Do

The Voices of Love

Rough winds do shake the darling buds of May

(Shakespeare: Sonnet xviii)

Our written language lasts as long as 'men can breathe, or eyes can see,' however changeable or transitory is nature or life. In Shakespeare's 'eternal lines', loveliness exists forever (ibid).

* * *

My approach to find the *naïve voice* is to set the scene visually and use very simple language to express feelings. My *wise voice* usually emerges from scribbles unbidden. For these writing exercises, I suggest tuning into the best of your adult self.

The Naïve Voice – use this style to:
- freewrite about Love
- write as the 'I' Voice of Love
- describe a loving scene
- write an unsent letter to someone you love or have loved
- write their imaginary reply to you

The Wise Voice – use this style to:
- freewrite about Love
- write as the 'I' Voice of Love
- describe a loving scene
- write an unsent letter to someone you love or have loved
- write their imaginary reply to you

Naïve & Wise Voices – using both voices:
- write a dialogue about Love
- write a dialogue about a loss of Love
- write a dialogue about who you love in the present

Dialogues

Write until a resolution or natural ending is reached
If you are finding your writing tedious, give yourself a time limit
Return another day, perhaps choosing one phrase as a starting point

The Naive Voice

This is an intuitive way of writing, best done through the moving of your pen or pencil on paper, or fingers on the keyboard, to let the words flow. Insights, I have found, come later and not necessarily immediately after the writing. Reflection has led me to the integration of child-like feelings within my adult self. I prefer child-like, rather than childish which feels a dismissive term to use for seriously real feelings.

Simple words and repetition really gets me into the feel of this naïve voice.

Write intuitively:

- use the present tense to bring your writing into the now

- experiment with punctuation, upper and lower case letters

- experiment with colour, fonts or handwriting

- experiment with finding child-like expressions / phrases / words

- play with the SIZE of words

- find the right length for your sentences: short

- find a really long way to express a really long thought with REALLY a **lot** of *words*

- repeating phrases works well

The Metaphor of Things

The Tao is an empty vessel; it is used, but never filled.
Oh, unfathomable source of ten thousand things!

"Verse Four" from *Tao Te Ching* by Lao Tsu trans.1972

The idea of ten thousand things suggests an infinite number and is often found in ancient Chinese philosophical texts. The poet Kathleen Raine uses the same concept in her poem *Amo Ergo Sum (Because I love):*
Ten thousand living things are sleeping in my arms.

Things provide metaphors. Metaphor makes it possible to say so much more than using language in a straightforward description for the invisible life of feelings. Finding the right metaphor is one of the arts of writing; it makes writing magical.

Reflections on two of the metaphors in *Love & Loss*:

Cup of Coffee in the Young Man Dream

When I wrote up the dream about the young man giving me a spectacular cup of coffee, it was a fun write, bringing a smile to my lips. A schmaltzy scene of boy meets girl came to mind from television adverts for instant coffee. Nevertheless the image of the dream young man took me on a long exploratory write which had far more gravitas. I had no idea where the writing was going to take me. Only in retrospect can I look back to see how the thread of the fun writing turned surprisingly into serious reflection.

Butterfly

The butterfly in the poem which ends the last chapter became a metaphor for love. An ideal choice because Love is never static. And the butterfly's life cycle is one of metamorphoses from egg to caterpillar, pupating into chrysalis, before emerging as an ephemeral butterfly with mosaic beautiful wings to fly freely. For some cultures, the butterfly symbolizes the eternal soul. The poetic use of the butterfly as metaphor is used by scientists in chaos theory with the esoteric hypothesis that the flapping of a butterfly's wings in one part of the globe may cause a hurricane a few weeks later somewhere else. The initial effects of falling in love may also create a maelstrom of emotions. Some of that varied emotional weather has found its way onto the pages of this book.

CHAPTER 5

Reflections on Love

Writing about Love has changed my awareness of its energetic force. My feelings and thoughts now pivot around Love as an energy ebbing and flowing through me towards others. And flowing in a similar way from others towards me. *Expressive and exploratory* writing in different styles has deepened and broadened how I embrace Love.

I have taken my time to finish this second mini-book. And I have particularly noted when my writing has been influenced from a meditative place, becoming aware of breath and stillness which have helped find the right word or phrase. I have felt an interaction of three elements in my body working together as I wrote: brain, heart and guts.

Does Love hold me or do I hold Love? That became a question I have tried to answer in this book. Have I found out a truth? Or may I find a Yes to both parts of that question which I leave hanging above the page?

Writing, whether on paper or the screen, is always my companion: a dialogue with myself in the first instance, helping me evolve as a human being. And my relationships with others, on whatever level, appear to improve, feel better and mature alongside this process. Much of my journal writing focuses on those I love, and dilemmas with which I tussle. Writing about love clarifies how to love each person in a way appropriate to that relationship, whoever they are.

Writing achieves a synthesis and integration of myself. In my real world of relationships, I have had extraordinary things happen as a result of my writing. As if writing with no anticipation of consequences in the material world does indeed lead to another level of reality. During one winter, just a week after finishing the poem: *Good-Bye Kisses* (see pp. 37-38) I received a Christmas card from the ex-lover making contact with me after a very long gap in any communication. Mysterious. Since then, we have met once and are able to keep very loosely in touch, giving me a completion, a rounded feeling, a rightness.

The retrospective panoramic appraisal of my heart is a benefit of getting older, particularly as I am now in my late sixties. In the first two thirds of my life, my heart held sway and led me to places which I have never regretted but periodically caused turmoil. Much of my early writing focussed on the embarrassments and disappointments love had brought me.

As a child I mistrusted the love I was told my parents felt for each other and found love unreliable as I became an adult (see p. 61). I had grown up with conditional love, heavy with criticism. I was also confused as I knew I was loved as a daughter, but not for the girl I was to become, nor for the woman I became later. Love had far more to do with duty than appreciation.

When I re-read my own writing I almost feel that my losses in love happened to someone else. I am long released from the pain of any of my past and particular loves. Although I have no difficulty remembering the urgency to write my feelings onto the page. But the writing in *Love & Loss* belongs to the past, as part of the pattern of my loving and definitely true to my life. All the writing has calmed me, although I certainly was not calm in those years of capturing my feelings in poems and prose. I have come to terms with the lost loves, and live in the presence of new loves.

This book started with a dream young man. Nevertheless I am finding the significance of the dream from six years ago and the exploratory writing afterwards is having long lasting consequences, belonging to the present in 2017. I am experiencing a sharpened awareness of how the meaning from this dream has transformed my everyday life.

In the village where I live, I go to a regular dance session: Open Floor.* With guidance from Sarah our teacher, every dancer explores their own free flowing movement and rhythm. We are of all ages and experience and dancing in this way allows each of us to express ourselves through movement. I find the physical, spiritual and emotional embodiment of the dancing the perfect match to my writing practice, and I write about any insights I have had afterwards.

At the end of one session I sat next to a younger man in the closing circle and said: *thank you for your young man energy.* And *thank you for your energy,* he replied immediately. Through this dancing community, young men and women have become part of my real life. Through the energy of the writing and now this dance class I feel a new zest infusing my life-force.

And as I go forward with this book, the daughter I gave birth to thirty years ago has in turn given birth to her own little boy. I shall discover what sort of love my grandson will bring into the world. Our love will go forward with a new generation, a new family formation.

Families are the places where love starts as well as the laying down of all sorts of emotions. The family is where we learn to relate, to copy behaviour and where we may rebel.

My next mini-book is called: *Shifting Boundaries*
(dealing with family scenarios, friendships and boundaries)

Appendix I

NOTES
* marked by an asterix in the text

INTRODUCTION

Georg Wilhelm Friedrich Hegel (1770–1831): German philosopher. In the early nineteenth century, he was considered to have conceived of the 'ultimate philosophical concept in the history of the Western mind.' Hegel's vision of reality transcended the previously accepted duality of thought. In every state is an opposite, he said, but then there is a third stage of integration between the two. Logically, this third state in turn would eventually become the basis for a further opposite and another synthesis.

(Tarnas 1991, pp. 379-83).

CHAPTER 1 – DREAM SNATCHER

Sigmund Freud was a vivid dreamer himself: his book *The Interpretation of Dreams* is a classic in the history of psychoanalysis. In the early years of the twentieth century, Freud encouraged his patients to free associate (also see Note p. 84) from the images in their dreams with the intention that this would lead him to insights, and an understanding of their problems. He analyzed his own dreams in exactly the same way. According to his biographer, *Freud very justly termed the interpretation of dreams the via regia to the unconscious.*   (Jones 1967, p. 300).

Carl Jung: see Notes for Chapter 2.

Dream Sharing: a good summary of the history of dreams, and a guide to the experience of sharing dreams, is given in *Dream Sharing* by Robin Shohet (1985, Turnstone Press).

Humanistic Psychotherapy: these are the therapies which evolved in the mid-twentieth century out of the psychoanalytic movement. The underlying principle and perspective is the potential of an individual to become a healthy and fulfilled person, who can make choices in life.

Gestalt Therapy: a term coined in 1950 and pioneered by Fritz Perls (1893–1970), an Austrian doctor who escaped Europe to settle in America. He lived, taught and introduced Gestalt Therapy at Esalen (on the Big Sur coastline of California, USA) in 1964. *Gestalt* meant 'whole' in his native German. His work transferred the meaning and interpretation of dreams to the dreamer, not the analyst or psychotherapist. Since those early days, Gestalt Therapy has evolved and is used in much of modern psychotherapeutic practice. To learn more about the start of modern psychotherapies and the birth of the human potential movement at the Esalen Institute see: www.esalen.org.

Animus: (inner masculine qualities for women) & **Anima:** (inner feminine qualities for men). For more understanding and the background to Carl Jung's interpretations see: Jung, E. (1978) *Animus and Anima*. Zurich: Spring Publications.

Built-in Orderly Organized Knowledge Device: a description with that title by Marielle Cartier, Alliance for Canada's Audio-Visual Heritage. URL: http://cool.conservation-us.org/byorg/abbey/an/an21/an21-8/an21-807.html. accessed: 17 June, 2017.

CHAPTER 2 – EROTIC ALERT

Dr Carl Jung (1875–1961): towards the end of his life, Jung was involved in writing a popular book to explain his ideas: *Man and his Symbols*. Jung broke with Freud's overtly narrow theories of sexuality and neuroses. His own concepts were far wider, stretching into many fields beyond medicine. There are 'innumerable things' he said 'beyond the range of human understanding' and his work as a psychoanalyst led him to find bridges in the human psyche between the conscious and unconscious nature of the mind. Followers of Carl Jung still find his psychoanalytical concepts powerful ideas to use in their thinking. Although many contemporary practitioners may take issue with his ideas about women.

Archetype: an abstract universal and archaic concept without form. Its roots lie in the concept of Plato's *Idea (eidos)*. Jung used this word to explain how an unconscious pattern underpins a meaning or an image. Each culture will make conscious through a recognizable form in art and stories, the archetypal behaviour of their age. Archetypes appear in myth and fairy tales right through to contemporary culture. The archetypal figure provides a powerful motif such as the great mother, father, child, the wise old man or woman, the trickster. The figure provided, however, is not the archetype but the material manifestation of the archetype. The idea of the archetype is essentially abstract and fluid.

Singer, J: the quote about the masculine and feminine principle came from a radio interview, which is no longer accessible. www.nautus.com/2007/04/an-interview-with-june-singer. accessed: 9 March 2012 via the Nautis Project.

Androgyny: June Singer revised her book on *Androgyny* at the end of the eighties with a new introduction explaining that her use of the word was as an archetype, not a social phenomenon. At that time, the expression of ambiguous sexuality was exploding on the scene of popular culture. In our current age, another wave of gender identity is making itself known in transgender and non-binary terms. Singer wrote in the preface to this second edition that actual gender identity was far from the intention of her ideas. She perceived androgyny as 'a consistent core idea that expresses itself in a variety of images and behaviours' depending on the culture in which they exist. Her work was about 'the separation of the inner opposites and the challenge to reunite them in a harmonious way.' My own use and understanding of the term is in that spirit too.

D.H. Lawrence (1885–1930): many consider Lawrence to be one of the giants of twentieth century literature. As a young man, however, his reputation in England was tarnished by general society who viewed his published works, which revealed the hidden nature of human sexual activity for both men and women, as shocking and vulgar. Some of his books were censored, and in cases banned in Britain for their explicit handling of language and sensuality. Lawrence eloped and then lived with the German wife of his professor from Nottingham University. In 1914 Frieda and Lawrence married, but by now it was the First World War and they were hounded by the military with accusations of spying. Long after his death, in the seventies, Lawrence was criticized by feminists like Kate Millet (1934–2017) who scorned his 'phallic consciousness' (1981 p. 238). These views have been rescinded by later academic women, critics like Catherine Brown (see: www.catherinebrown.org Blog posted on 3 September, 2014 – accessed 10 February 2017).

The Snake: one of the world's most potent symbols with many different interpretations. The snake has fed into mythologies reaching far back into antiquity in continents as far apart as Africa, India and the Americas. The rod of Asclepius, the Greek god of healing, has a snake entwined around a stick and is the principal symbol for medicine. Some motifs come from its ability to coil and uncoil; or side-wind from east to west as it glides along the ground from north to south.

Still Point: a term used by cranial osteopaths to describe a pause in the fluctuations and rhythms of cerebrospinal fluids which influences healing and rebalancing in the body.

Chakra: a vortex of life-force energy at points along the axis of the spine. The word *chakra* means a wheel in Sanskrit. The solar plexus is just above the navel in the centre of the body (Rendel 1974, p. 10).

Gerda Boyesen (1922–2005): a pioneering Norwegian psychotherapist and founder of Biodynamic Psychology. Originally a clinical psychologist, then with a training in physiotherapy and massage, she developed a subtle way of working with the body, emotions and mind. London became her home in 1968; later she opened her first training centre, as well as teaching all over the world.

Shadow: a Jungian term meaning the dark side of the personality – what is denied, inferior, unacceptable, negative and buried from the conscious self. When repressed *the shadow* may act in destructive ways.

Synchronicity: a Jungian term meaning a coincidence of two phenomena which are not connected but become meaningful.

Collective Unconscious: another Jungian term, meaning a level of experience in every human being which appears to be inherited, not learnt, and to be universal rather than personal. These could include imprinted characteristics that have evolved from ancestral and archaic memories. Examples might be symbols of rebirth in religious or spiritual belief systems, or a primitive and instinctive fear of snakes or spiders.

Freewriting: a phrase and technique devised by Peter Elbow, Professor of English Emeritus at the University of Massachusetts, USA. He developed this approach to his own writing of academic essays in the fifties, as he was struggling to write at all. It worked and he went on to teach it to others. Freewriting is now widely accepted within creative writing circles.

Free association: the original technique that Freud used with his patients when listening to their dreams. He encouraged them to talk spontaneously about the images and thoughts which came into their minds. He believed this would lead the patient to uncover repressed feelings and events. In that way Freud would be led to understand the unconscious root of their problems. He used self-analysis on himself which helped him understand his patients better.

CHAPTER 3 – THE RAW HEART

Exhibition: *Edvard Munch by Himself* at The Royal Academy of Arts in 2005.

Punctuation: Timothy Dexter (1747–1806) was an uneducated, eccentric businessman from Massachusetts who had an uncanny aptitude for making money. He wrote a memoir: *A Price for the Knowing Ones* with no punctuation in it at all. It became popular and in the second edition, he added a page of punctuation at the end for readers to 'peper and solt it as they plese.' (Truss 2007, pp. ix-x). Also see: *The Strange Life of 'Lord' Timothy Dexter* by Zachary Crockett. www.priceconomics.com accessed: 7 March, 2017.

Projection: a Freudian concept when one person holds emotions and thoughts, but denies these feelings belong to themselves, and unconsciously transfers them onto another individual.

Tulla Larsen pursued Munch after the end of an affair. Behind closed doors, so no-one knows the actual truth, an argument arose. A gun was shot and one of Munch's fingers (of his palette-holding left hand) was shattered which was to cause him pain for the rest of his life.

The Scream: apparently Munch wrote: *for several years I was almost mad . . . you know my picture, The Scream, I was stretched to the limit – nature was screaming in my blood. After that I gave up hope ever of being able to love again.* http://www.artlyst.com accessed 16 April, 2012. The first of four versions, painted in 1895, was on display before a sale at Sothebys, London in April 2012. I visited on the 17 April. The painting sold for the record sum, at the time, of £73.9m.

Attraction: dry point on copperplate (1905).

Abyssinia was the old name for Ethiopia and covered a vast territory in ancient times. According to historical and literary legend which has passed down the centuries, the Queen of Sheba may have travelled through the desert across these lands. Modern Ethiopia is much more compact, so it is not exactly clear where this might have been.

Ekphrasis: derived from the Greek words, *ek* and *phrasis*, 'out' and 'speak'. For an explanatory piece about ekphrastic writing see poet Abegail Morley's work with her students (11 October, 2013). https://abegailmorley.wordpress.com/2013/10/11/ekphrasis/ (accessed: 16 March, 2017).

Font: the word is derived from *fonderie* (Old French), the modern French word *fondre* and the English word *foundry* all have their derivation in the meaning to melt or cast in metal (OED). The sixteenth century invention of the printing press, with movable letters cast in metal, revolutionized how the written word was reproduced. Now every computer comes with a pre-loaded choice of fonts.

CHAPTER 4 – BUTTERFLY

Attachment Theory: developed by Dr. John Bowlby (1907–1990) in the mid-1950s. He wanted to understand the impact early social development of infants had on their childhood and adult behaviour. Attachment theory has been influential in shaping developmental psychology. In more recent years, neuroscientists have taken up and researched more about how the brain develops after birth and linked this to the early care received by babies.

CHAPTER 5 – REFLECTIONS ON LOVE

Open Floor Dancing: evolved from Gabrielle Roth's 5Rhythms work. The flow of this dancing is a movement meditation practice, underpinned with the same intentions as creative therapeutic writing: deep healing, creative expression and finding the authentic self (www.waveofenergy.co.uk).

RESOURCE

Lapidus International – The Words for Wellbeing Association promotes the benefits of writing and reading and has members throughout the UK and abroad. The web-site will provide links to other relevant organisations and networks in the field.

www.lapidus.org.uk

Appendix II

WRITING STYLES AND THEMES

Voices, Wise, Naïve and Lyrical   *Chapter 4*
Dialogue, Child-like and Adult Self
Love, Baby and Attachment Theory
Writing, Nurturing and Security
Metaphor and Butterfly
New Love as a Gift

References

Bolton, G. (2014). *The Writer's Key Introducing Creative Solutions for Life*. London: Jessica Kingsley Publishers.

Boyesen, G. (1976). *The Primary Personality and its Relationship to the Streamings* in *In The Wake of Reich* edited by David Boadella. London: Coventure Ltd.

Briggs, P. (2005). *Ethiopia*. Bucks: Bradt Travel Guides.

Cartier, M. (1997). *Built-in Orderly Organized Knowledge Device*. Abbey Newsletter. Volume 21, Number 8. accessed: 8 April 2017.

Elbow, P. [1973] (1998). *Writing Without Teachers*. New York: Oxford University Press.

Jones, E. [1953] (1967). *The Life and Work of Sigmund Freud*. London: Pelican Books.

Jung, C.G. (1959). *The Archetypes and the Collective Unconscious: Volume Nine, Part 1*. translated by F.C. Hull. London: Routledge & Kegan Paul.

Jung, C.G. (1964). *Man and his Symbols*. London: Aldus Books.

Jung, E. (1978). *Animus and Anima*. Zurich: Spring Publications.

Garfield, S. (2010). *Just My Type – A Book About Fonts*. London: Profile Books.

Greer, G. (2003). *The Boy*. London: Thames & Hudson.

Lao Tsu (trans. 1972, Gia-Fu Feng and Jane English). *Tao Te Ching*. London: Wildwood House.

Lawrence, D.H. (1923). *Snake* in *Stories, Essays and Poems*. London: Dent.

Millet, K. (1981) [1969]. *Sexual Politics*. London: Virago Press.

Perls, F. (1971). *Gestalt Therapy Verbatim*. New York: Bantam Books.

Prideaux, S. (2005). *Edward Munch Behind The Scream*. New Haven and London: Yale University Press.

Raine, K. (1985) [1952]. *Amo Ergo Sum* in *The Bloodaxe Book of Contemporary Women Poets* (ed: Jeni Couzyn). Newcastle upon Tyne: Bloodaxe Books.

Rendel, P. (1974). *Introduction To The Chakras*. Northamptonshire: The Aquarian Press.

Singer, J. [1976] (1989). *Androgyny The Opposites Within*. Boston: Sigo Press.

Shohet, R. (1985). *Dream Sharing*. Wellingborough: Turnstone Press.

Tarnas. R. (1991). *The Passion of the Western Mind*. London: Pimlico.

Truss, L (2007). *Eats, Shoots & Leaves The Zero Tolerance Approach to Punctuation*. London: Profile Books.

Turner-Vesselago, B. (2013). *Writing Without a Parachute: The Art of Freefall*. London: Jessica Kingsley Publishers.

Warland, B. (2010). *Breathing The Page: Reading The Act of Writing*. Toronto: Cormorant Books Inc.

Watson, B. (trans 1968). *The Complete Works of Chuang Tzu*. New York: Columbia University Press.

Zohar, D. (1990). *The Quantum Self*. London: Bloomsbury.

Index

Boxes for Exercises or Information are in bold

for your own notes
and scribbles

for your own notes
and scribbles

for your own notes
and scribbles

A Fox Crossed My Path

creative therapeutic writing on a depressive illness

The first mini-book in the series:

A Fox Crossed My Path explores how writing aids recovery and integration of the Ill Self and the Well Self.

For anyone with an interest in the therapeutic potential of expressive and creative writing, *A Fox Crossed My Path* is a find. Like spending time with a good novel or short story, this book leaves the reader changed, more aware of how people's lives are, and this life in particular. I would suggest that for starting points in how creative writing can be a life-line when other options are limited, this book is a must-read.

Jeannie Wright

Self & Society – An International Journal for Humanistic Psychology
Vol. 45 October 2017 pp. 337-338.

* Buy *A Fox Crossed My Path*

* Respond to *Love & Loss*

* Enquiries about Readings or Presentations

www.monicasuswin.com

ISBN 978-0-9956882-0-9